The Sandwich

The Sandwich

Faith, hope, love and why things are still OK.

Glenn Myers

Copyright © 2021 Glenn Myers
Version 1.0

First published 2021 by Fizz Books

GlennMyers.info

ISBN 978-0-9565010-8-0 (paperback)
ISBN 978-0-9565010-7-3 (epub)

Glenn Myers has asserted his right under the Copyright, Designs and Patents Act 1988 to be identified as the author of this work.

Scriptures taken from the Holy Bible, New International Version®, NIV®. Copyright © 1973, 1978, 1984, 2011 by Biblica, Inc.™ Used by permission of Zondervan. All rights reserved worldwide. www.zondervan.com The "NIV" and "New International Version" are trademarks registered in the United States Patent and Trademark Office by Biblica, Inc.™

Cover design by Chris Lawrence

Apart from any use permitted under UK copyright law, this publication may only be reproduced, stored or transmitted, in any form, or by any means, with prior permission in writing of the publishers or, in the case of reprographic production, in accordance with the terms of licences issued by the Copyright Licensing Agency.

British Library Cataloguing in Publication Data
A CIP catalogue for this book is available from the British Library
Printed by Ingram, Milton Keynes MK11 3LW, UK.

Contents

Author's note 7

Foreword 9

The solution to all our problems
How if we took the worst from each denomination, we could decline much faster 11

Anointed
How we love the hyperbolic 15

No escape
How frustration and losing your mind is part of the package 19

Learning good sense from small children
How thinking like they do, helps 25

Fate and Luck
Escaping from their supervision 31

On heroes
About how you just can't get them or be them 37

Hearing wrongly from God
About how putting your hands over your ears may impair your hearing 41

Unfair competition?
How it's OK to have megachurches 45

The God that trusts
About how being trusted feels just like being abandoned 51

The practical challenges of being an angel
About finding the right broom tree, virgin, apostle, or musical note 57

The prayer meeting
About how God wants us naked, but we keep reaching for our clothes. 63

The empty nest
The hole truth 69

The biggest failure in the Bible
How it happened 77

Praying for miracles
About the sun rising again 85

On soulmates
About how they sound like a good idea 91

'God's not fair'
About riding forth for justice on a small horse 99

What I learnt from nearly dying
Where to invest 105

Prayerlessness
About catching the moment 111

Shallowness
How to master looking good on an empty soul 117

'I never knew you'
About not living on fumes 123

Let it be
About the tangle of free will and love, and the weakness of God. 129

And finally 135

About the author 136

AUTHOR'S NOTE

I worked in the youthful city of Singapore in the early 1990s on the editorial team of *Impact* magazine. *Impact* offered teaching in Christian discipleship for the thousands of people joining the churches in that city state.

I was sometimes asked to write for *Impact* after we returned to the UK following our two-year stint, and those two years have lengthened into almost 20. I'm so grateful to Andrew Goh and the *Impact* team for their encouragement (and royalties) over the years.

This book is an edited collection of my favourites from all those articles. I noticed that I kept revisiting the same space, the place in a Christian's head where God's promises and life's routines meet and where we can respond to disappointment and difficulty with false notes or true ones.

Back in the UK our own kids grew up. We repaid the mortgage. I suffered life-changing health challenges. We stayed married. It's fun (for me) to watch my writing be shaped by all this. The kids who are mentioned in some of these pieces are now all growed up, one is producing children of her own, and they both make us feel very proud.

I'm still excited by the hope of the Kingdom of God. Through all these years I've watched fellow Christians live the same lives as everyone else, start to sag with the same wrinkles, host the same sicknesses, but yet cultivate (many of them) things that elude others - a patience, a generosity, a peaceableness, a quiet order, a capacity for delight. It's

The sandwich

natural to want these things for yourself and to explore how to get them. Hence this book. I hope you find it fun and provocative.

Thanks ...

To Andrew and our fellow-toilers at *Impact* over the years; to the wider Christian community in Singapore who were such a blessing and encouragement; to friends who read this final manuscript and offered comments and criticism, especially Andrew Bowker, Jude Simpson and Andy Chamberlain; to Chris Lawrence for again coming up with a great cover; and, as ever, to Cordelia and our offspring.

FOREWORD

Writing that refreshes. That's what Glenn Myers does with glee.

It may not appear in the immediate but you would be halfway through the second cup before you realize you have drunk deeply from his wicked sense of humour and astounding craftsmanship.

Here is a wordsmith par excellence. Often one would pause and remark silently, "now, that's a good choice of word or expression". So, whether it is recalling a homely incident or an event from the international stage, Glenn is a master at teasing and pleasing. He has some strong views for such a genial-looking person. But he presents them cogently and persuasively, almost like a back-handed compliment; not forcing anything down anyone's throat. He is respectful of his readers and invites them for a congenial mental sparring rather than a knock-out blow.

When he shares the Good News of the Gospel and spiritual matters, he comes across as authentic and heart-warming. Glenn has a powerful message and conveys it winsomely.

Andrew Goh, Editor, *Impact* Magazine, Singapore.

THE SOLUTION TO ALL OUR PROBLEMS

How if we took the worst from each denomination, we could decline much faster
(1994)

I was fond of Singapore's multi-denominational scene, and the opportunity I had to lift the lid on various churches and peek inside. Fun fact: among those committed to Jesus, we're all similar under our denominational skin. I hope everyone will forgive me for the following.

What we need is a new denomination.

I visited a Brethren church the other day, for the first time for about fifteen years. Things hadn't changed much.

The church building still displayed the minimum possible aesthetic sense, designed (it wasn't hard to guess) by deacons, all male. They hadn't quite suppressed every splash of colour -- it's hard to completely stamp out human, and especially feminine, creativity -- but they were certainly subsisting on the bare minimum. The hall was 1930s hospital style: dull dark wood and magnolia. The most recent addition was a 1970s chipboard hymnbook cabinet with a balsa wood veneer (artificial). Brethren don't waste resources on Art.

We sang hymns, though, great eighteenth-century affairs loaded with fine doctrine like plum puddings. The singing was concerted, massive, and rousing -- marred only by a few sopranos warbling out of control, like opera

The sandwich

divas tumbling into the orchestra pit or stuka bombers that can't pull out of a fatal dive.

When the people on the platform addressed the Almighty, you rather got the impression of the serf, cap in hand, going to the landowner. These were Brethren. A people who know their place in the scheme of things.

I felt at home at once. Here were my roots. Plain but godly. 1930s decor and 1790s doggerel, sin and magnolia. Nothing changes here. Hardly anything, indeed, *had* changed, since I'd left these pastures for charismatic ones a decade and a half ago.

Singing solid hymns that fed the brain and spirit was a nice change from my current church, where -- as a contrast -- spiritual ecstasy is expected fifteen minutes into each service, whether or not you feel like it first thing in the morning and whether or not you've got a headache.

In our church, we do not all sing together. We play tag with the worship leader. You know the game. You're all ready for the second verse but he's jumped back to the middle of the chorus. Just when you think you're catching him again, he's onto a second lap with the first verse. The musicians and the 'waa waa' girls are not far behind, but he dodges them astutely when they start getting near. Finally he helps us by repeating the line 'He is worthy' seven straight times, until less charitable members of congregation want to knock him on the head to get the music into a different groove. We hit the seventh 'He is worthy' with a great bashing of drums, like a Taoist funeral, and then blast off into singing in tongues or a 'clap offering.'

The solution to all our problems

In my church, we are not so much serfs addressing the Lord of the Manor as people frantically cranking a Van de Graaf generator, hoping the sparks will crackle. I sometimes look round at the upturned faces and hands and wonder, *am I the only person in the church not enjoying this? Is anybody else -- like me -- faking it?*

Hmm. And yet the charismatics and Pentecostals are the most successful missionary movement in history: from a standing start in 1900 to 400 million plus today. God's at work among us. Sometimes -- despite everything -- the sparks do crackle.

Perhaps no denomination has it all. But I have the perfect way forward for the future: The Singapore Post-Denominational Church. We'll pick-and-mix from what the current denominations offer to produce an unforgettable ecclesiastical experience.

Here's my suggestions: We'll look to the Brethren for the art and aesthetics. Flexibility and ecumenism? Call in the Bible-Presbyterians. Theological rigour? Charismatic choruses are just the job. A due sense of tradition and history? The new independent churches will supply all we need.

I'll be the pastor, of course, and will lovingly fix my salary at an average of the top four pastoral renumerations in Singapore. Tithes will be high, but at least you'll know I'm safe from being headhunted and will be able to devote myself wholeheartedly to the Post-Denominational cause.

The sandwich

Singapore Post-Denominational Church. Come along next Sunday. I guarantee, after the experience, you'll love your own worship tradition all the more.

ANOINTED

How we love the hyperbolic
(1995)

As the only interdenominational Christian magazine in Singapore, we were the landing zone for many hopeful press releases. I enjoyed this part of the job. With some of them, though, I wondered if the copywriters hadn't been drinking a little too deeply of the marketing juice.

Sometimes you wonder.

We get lots of mail in the *Impact* office. Some of it is promotional. Here are some quotes from material lying around the office:

> *Pastor X is one of the strongest church leaders in the world today.*

> *A man with a strong apostolic and prophetic mantle, Pastor Y is impacting the world.*

> *Dr Z is one of the most anointed Bible teachers in the world.*

Here's a longer one describing someone's ministry in Japan and inviting funds for the school that trained him:

> *At first they came by the dozens.*

> *Then, they came by the hundreds*

The sandwich

And finally, they came by the thousands.

And they stream across the playing field of a 60,000 seat baseball stadium to commit their lives to Jesus Christ.

It gets better:

This is happening in the inscrutable orient -- in Japan, the country some have called the 'missionary graveyard'.

The report goes on:

Closed. Until now. What has changed?

Who is God using to lead thousands of Japanese to publicly turn their faces to the cross -- and their backs on centuries of religious tradition?

Aw, you guessed. A Japanese evangelist trained by the school.

The report fails to mention that responses like that were the normal pattern in Japan after World War II, and they were mostly for cultural reasons rather than spiritual ones. Japan's churches have remained small, less than 1% of the population, despite hundreds of thousands of responses in large evangelistic meetings. It is astonishing that the school didn't train its evangelists to understand

Anointed

this, and even more astonishing that they should be boasting about their ignorance of both history and culture.

Hype. A late-twentieth century disease entirely absent from the ministry of Jesus and the apostles. (Can you imagine it? 'Let's put our hands together and welcome Paul, acclaimed author of *Romans*, one of today's most anointed missionaries...') Chillingly present among the rag-tag-and-bobtail heretics who so damaged the Early Church.

Hype. There must be better ways for honest leaders with genuine ministries to promote what they're doing. Let us pray:

'From good people, doing good things, badly, Good Lord, deliver us.'

NO ESCAPE

How frustration and losing your mind is part of the package
(1996)

I wrote this shortly after my time at Impact, *but when we were still full-on with two small children (my son was born in Singapore). My now-grown-up daughter has produced children of her own so we get to have another go (and also get to lie down in a quiet room to recover). I have, by the way, managed to read nearly every copy of the* Economist *for the past quarter century.*

When I lived in Singapore, 1993-1995, I didn't work on Saturdays.

I often wished I did. I'd quite like to take up workaholism. It does a lot of good to your bank balance and people think you are a busy, important person.

Saturdays came round with a terrible frequency (one almost every week), more than one hundred over two years. Public holidays added to the load.

These off-days were our family days. And if the phrase 'family day' fosters the same anxiety and nervous tension in your heart as the phrase 'family service' does, then I conclude that you, too, are a father of toddlers.

Saturdays would start, of course, much like every other day: with the siren wail of my baby son calling through the pre-dawn gloom for Room Service. Thomas and I are at our best in mornings, unlike my wife and daughter, and so we were obliged to spend the time

The sandwich

together. Mostly, we spent it looking through the bars of our window across the road to Block 285, Thomas sitting in my arms, gazing out, smooth-skinned and tubby, like a Buddha.

Together, we would mark the passing of each quarter hour. First the strangled warble of the primary school's cockerel, at whom I often longed to aim a semi-automatic rifle. (It was he who woke Thomas up.) Next, the soothing rush-rush of the streetsweeper. After that, the taxi driver starting his engine, switching on his lights, pausing for a thoughtful moment and then swishing out in search of prey on Avenue 2. Shortly after 6.30, we'd hear the *clack clack* of the heels of a slim office worker, in search of a feeder bus. And at last came the sunrise.

Cornflakes normally followed all this. Our three-year-old daughter would join us, and I would take a cup of strong tea to my wife. 'Come on,' I would say, 'I definitely want one eyelid open.' On normal days, on good days, this was now the cue to get ready for work -- blessed work!-- and walk out the door. On Saturdays it was not so.

Like a bad day in Death Valley

My sister had visited once from England and rashly bought the children a plastic Wendy house, big enough to sit in. I came to view it with a sort of horror. Ruth, my daughter, was fond of hosting birthday parties there for her favourite doll, Dotty. Dotty is a rag of a toy, hair a mess, clearly a doll with toddlers of her own, unlike the well-groomed bimbos you find perched in ski suits on the shelves of Toys 'R' Us.

No escape

I liked Dotty. Yanked, as she was, around the flat by her hair, stuffed into toy prams, left for dead when more interesting things came along, I thought she and I would have much to talk about. But her birthdays did come round rather often.

'Here's some cake for you, Daddy.'

'How marvellous.' An empty plastic plate. Inside the Wendy house it is at least 46 degrees and rising.

'It's a birthday cake, for Dotty's birthday.'

'Yum Yum'

'She's four.'

'I'm glad to hear it.'

'And what else would you like to eat?'

'Er, I don't know.'

'We've got crisps, sausages, cheese, eggs or char siew pau'

'Crisps please.'

I knew what I really wanted. On the table, pages rustling lightly in the breeze from the fan, would be my freshly printed copy of *The Economist*. I would like to take it to the hawker centre and order roti prata and coffee and sit down and munch and read all about British politics and be happy. Taking part in Dotty's birthday celebrations in

The sandwich

a plastic tent in Ruth's room that felt like midday in Death Valley formed no part of my plans.

'I think there's a wolf outside,' said Ruth.

'A wolf! Definitely. Let me chase it off.' At least when you fight wolves there's oxygen to breathe.

There's always books

When it wasn't Dotty's birthday, and when the wolves were friendly, or only little, there were, of course, books. This could be fun for a while, like when someone gave us the same Ladybird edition of 'The Elves and the Shoemaker' that my mum or dad had read to me, setting off long-forgotten resonances in my mind from thirty years before.

Alas, I found that even the best children's book pales a bit after the dozenth reading. And before we left Singapore we had read 'The Tale of Peter Rabbit' so many times that Ruth knew the first forty-six pages by heart. We had followed James the Red Engine and the Troublesome Trucks up Gordon's Hill more times than I cared to think about. I began to long for Postman Pat to drive his Bright Red Van right over his blasted Black-and-White Cat and be arrested by PC Selby for dangerous driving. Some books we actually hid so that the children didn't find them.

Money and technology

We did, of course, wonder frequently if there wasn't a better solution to all of this. This is nearly the twenty-first century. Throwing money and technology at a

No escape

problem is usually thought to solve it. And solutions were offered at every hand.

● We once saw a baby's cot fitted with a voice-activated electronic rocker. No sooner does Junior squawk after a bad dream than the machinery kicks in.

● Or there are videos and children's TV. We did even tackle one issue in my time at *Impact* on the lines of 'Is it OK just to show my children Christian videos all day?' We thought not, but we were tempted.

● Or rent a maid, or stuff our children's little blonde heads with Mandarin and Maths in the name of good parenting.

No doubt all that can help. But it didn't finally solve the problem. It's us the little brutes want.

T-I-M-E

I sometimes wonder what sort of a Father God is. A failure, by many counts. Most of his progeny, humans, avoid him. They snack freely from his larder but don't want to listen to or talk to him or give him joy in his old age: an unfilial lot.

They must drive him crazy. He anguishes over them. He occasionally admits to not knowing what to do with them. It would be nice for God, you would think, to put humans into childcare and spend a happy Saturday calling a few new Universes into existence.

Yet it seems that God can never quite rid himself of his curious idea about what Fatherhood should be: love

The sandwich

them and give yourself for them. Disregarding the cost, the anguish, the boredom, he lowers himself into our Wendy houses and listens to our chatter.

Perhaps he's right. Despite tutoring, toys and TV, our children still seem to spell love T-I-M-E. No-one but us -- grumpy, distracted us -- will do. I'm the only daddy my daughter's got. Me being there makes her happy. There's no escape.

I suppose *The Economist* will still be there when my children are all gone. So will my Saturdays. I might even, in time, come to miss the Wendy house.

LEARNING GOOD SENSE FROM SMALL CHILDREN

How thinking like they do, helps
(1997)

Another article written with kids roaming outside my study door, shepherded usually by my wife.

> *Anyone who will not receive the kingdom of God like a little child will never enter it (Mark 10:15)*

> *Christ said we must become as little children to enter the Kingdom of heaven. Dear God, this is too much. Have we got to become such idiots? (Protestant reformer Martin Luther, c. 1538)*

Talking bananas

Our children normally have a banana for breakfast and I have got into the habit of ringing it up before we eat it.

'do-dee-der-dee-der-der-der

'-Ring-

'Hello, are you a banana?

'Yes

'Would you like to be eaten today?

The sandwich

'Oh, alright then.

'OK Thanks! Bye'

Presumably this little game will one day cease to be entertaining for the kids in the morning. (I hope quite soon.)

However, I was doing this one morning recently when my five-year-old daughter suddenly spoke up.

'It's not the banana talking at all! It's you!'

I looked at her out of the corner of my eye, Has she only just realized this? I thought. Has she thought all these months and years that you can ring bananas up? And that they talk back? I wondered what else was going on, unsuspected by me, between her ears.

'You're right' I admitted. 'It's me.'

Wet and wild

I work from home, in an upstairs room overlooking our garden, so I sometimes get to watch our three-year-old playing on his own: tramping about in his red wellies (rubber boots), watering the plants, digging in the sandpit. He shovels out sand and heaps it into his tractor. He collects stones in a bucket. He stirs the sand round and round with a stick, all the time talking. 'Mum, I'm a collector. I'm collecting things.' 'Mum, I'm baking a cake. It's a chocolate cake. With lemons.' His mind, I observe, seems like a home you've just moved into: all the furniture's there, but it hasn't been straightened out quite yet.

Learning good sense from small children

In his book *Queen of Angels*, science fiction writer Greg Bear writes about an age when psychotherapy and computer modelling are so advanced that therapists will be able to take computer-aided journeys round the landscape of people's minds, investigating the country and solving deep traumas.

Brilliant and daring though he is, he never speculates on the insides of a child's mind. I can imagine why: it's too wild. Certainly my kids' minds are like that, mad, happy tea-parties where disconnected ideas and talking bananas jostle together.

It can't be true

A child's mindset is interesting in the same way the roller-coaster ride called Space Mountain in Euro-Disney outside Paris is interesting: riding it you're completely in the dark and you don't know where you're going to be thrown next.

But it's also interesting because, as we know, a child's mind is a holy thing, a thing we must emulate if we are to get in on the kingdom of God. A child's mind is nearer to the kingdom of God than a grownup's. How can this be? Here are two ideas:

Wonder. Children know about wonder; grownups have to relearn it. Remember the answer Jesus gave to John the Baptist's question, 'Are you the one that was sent?': the Lord Jesus told the questioners 'The blind receive sight, the lame walk, those who have leprosy are cured, the dead are raised, and the good news is preached to the poor.' (Luke 7:22). 'No eye has seen, no ear has heard, no mind has conceived what God has prepared for

The sandwich

those who love him,' says the apostle Paul (1 Cor 2:9). 'Dear friends, *now* we are children of God,' adds John, 'and what we will be has not yet been made known.' (1 John 3:2).

According to the New Testament, we are seeing the first, outriding snowballs of goodness tumbling down heaven's mountainside into our lives; an avalanche will follow. As Christians we have every reason to develop a childlike capacity for wonder. Outrageous, lovely things really do happen. The future will be rich with them.

Relationship. Children have the enviable ability to have their problems solved with a hug. As grownup Christians we think a hug is not enough. But it is enough. 'Peace I leave with you,' says the Lord Jesus, 'Do not let your hearts be troubled and do not be afraid' (John 14:27). 'Do not be anxious about anything,' says Paul, shockingly; instead, 'present your requests to God. And the peace of God, which transcends all understanding, will guard your hearts and minds in Christ Jesus' (Phil 4: 6-7).

It is characteristic of Jesus that in the toughest times he does not explain things. Instead, he showers us with love and peace. It isn't (rational, modern) explanation or (shrugging, post-modern) escapism we need; it is enough to be loved. Children know it; adults forget it.

At the heart of the Universe -- we need to remember-- is not a series of laws, nor something blind and chaotic, but a Good Person whom we do well to know (as children easily accept). His normal speech is what we call the laws

Learning good sense from small children

of universe; his special words of love are what we call signs and wonders; fail to see him and we miss everything.

Maybe we should not be so committed to edifices of adult thought. Maybe the foolish playfulness of God, the God of talking bananas, is a surer foundation. We need the playful mind of a child to keep up with the rampant gaiety of a good God. Try this song as a quick summary of all we need to know (though in our case sung to Jesus rather than to a lover):

'I don't believe in many things, but in You, I do, I do.

FATE AND LUCK
Escaping from their supervision
(2003)

Many Singaporeans were first- or second-generation Christians and Chinese traditional religion was the primaeval soup from which they emerged. A Chinese traditional religionist might see Christianity as (just) another temple from which you might get temporary blessings -- but your Fate will still be your Fate. Luck, too, seemed important among some Singaporean Chinese just it is as among superstitious types (such as sports fans) in my home country. The Chinese character '8' is particularly lucky and it wasn't a coincidence that the Beijing Olympics, that nervous moment of global exposure for mainland China, started on 8:08pm on 8/8/2008. It was fun to try to learn about Luck and Fate in the light of the Bible.

You can think of them as people. Luck is female: tall, pale, beautiful, elusive. When you don't expect it, she flashes you a warm smile. But try to get friendly, and she's gone. One moment you're dancing with her; the next, you're dancing alone.

Fate is male, thuggish and not very subtle. You see him shoving through the crowds. He takes you by the collar. 'Don't do that.' He growls. 'Do this.'

Does faith make you lucky?
But surely our faith will charm and tame Luck and Fate?

We read in our Bibles that 'goodness and love will follow me all the days of my life' (Psalm 23:6).

The sandwich

And common sense makes us think, too, that on the whole, Christians will probably endure less than the average serving of 'bad luck'. For example, just as I was writing this article, I (luckily) found that two Christian newspapers in the UK had recently been writing about luck. They had commissioned a survey of attitudes and given the results to a psychologist who specialised in understanding psychological factors in creating luck. He found that, compared with the average person, committed Christians will be luckier, because Christians tend to:

- Chat to strangers (so they will have more happy coincidences with meeting people)
- Expect other people to be helpful and friendly (which is often self-fulfilling)
- Expect bad situations to produce good in the end (which has the effect of helping you reap the best from any given situation.)

Then, it seems to me that Christians are less likely to be involved in some risky or unwise behaviour, which also affects your 'luck'. Here in the UK, many traffic accidents, diseases, and crimes arise out of alcohol abuse, clubbing, smoking, drugs and gambling. It is rotten luck to be hit by a drunken driver. But this rotten luck is more likely to happen at times in the night when the Christians are already self-righteously tucked up in bed with some hot cocoa and the latest copy of the *Church Times*, safely protected from sinners.

True, you may spill your cocoa and be badly burnt, or you may be angry at some *Church Times* article and suffer a stroke and die. There is, indeed, a finite probability that you will first burn yourself with cocoa and

Fate and Luck

then suffer a stroke and die because of the *Church Times.* But still, rest assured, snug in bed, you are safer and luckier than the average.

Oh no, it doesn't

So – to repeat the question -- does the Christian faith charm and tame Luck and Fate?

Not so fast. Christianity has side-effects that might look 'lucky'. But waving prayers and Bible promises at those evil characters Fate and Luck is about as much use as waving a child's plastic sword or cardboard shield at Death itself.

Let's not be shallow. Look around in your church. You will see people suffering from the most outrageous, improbable acts of bad luck or malicious fate. If you personally have escaped so far, stick around. Never think, just because your life is going well, that the Christian faith has finally persuaded Luck to fall in love with you or Fate to tone down the bad stuff. Remember the same book of Psalms that contains the promise

Surely your goodness and love will follow me all the days of my life (Psalm 23:6)

also contains Psalm 13, which is rarely quoted on Christian-themed cards:

How long, LORD? Will you forget me
for ever?
How long will you hide your face
from me? How long must I wrestle
with my thoughts

The sandwich

*and day after day have sorrow in
my heart?
How long will my enemy triumph
over me? (vv1-2)*

Quit the game

I'm not sure that Christianity is really much use for manipulating Luck or Fate. Why? *Because that's not what the Christian faith is for.*

Take the apostle Paul. Before his conversion to Christ, he was a clever, well-educated, hard-working, zealous, and highly respectable young man, from a good family, the sort every Jewish mother might want for her daughter.

Conversion ruined this promising, respectable life. Paul abandoned a good career as a Pharisee and rising politician and instead travelled the world preaching the gospel. From then on, his was almost a cursed life. Wherever he went, trouble followed. He kept being flogged. Mobs attacked him. City authorities despaired of him. He was in and out of jail. At times, people prophesied that he was fated for trouble if he visited Jerusalem. He went anyway. Sometimes, riots happened despite his best efforts, just through 'bad luck'. He was kept in jail in Caesarea for two years as an innocent man on the careless whim of a corrupt governor: what a rotten stroke of luck. He didn't care.

He had turned to Christ. Life then seemed to turn on him. And yet he never turned back. Why? Because when he turned to Christ, Paul had found Life Himself. He

Fate and Luck

found the Priceless Pearl, and he gave up everything else to get it.

Before his conversion, Paul's religion could have been described as 'principles for a successful life.' But they didn't work for him: they were fine principles, but there was no power. After he met Christ, life became about being joined to The Life, loving Him, serving Him, bearing His fruit. He gave up, in a sense, on wisdom for living and preferred to die every day.

And Fate and Luck no longer had any power over him. Bring 'em on. Let them do their worst: they only became something like allies in his pursuit of God.

In one of the most famous chapters of his most famous book, Paul wrote,

> *... we boast in the hope of the glory of God. Not only so, but we also glory in our sufferings, because we know that suffering produces perseverance; perseverance, character; and character, hope (Romans 5:2-4).*

It's as if he said, 'Good luck? Well, if heaven drops a date, I'll open my mouth. Bad luck? That will just drive me deeper into the resources of Jesus.'

Paul's co-authors on the Christian textbook agree. Here's James: Trials? The testing of my faith develops perseverance. Peter: Trials? They just prove my faith genuine, like a storm proves the seaworthiness of great

The sandwich

ship. Even the writer of Psalm 13, I found, eventually takes his eye off himself and his rotten luck and focuses on the eternal. Never mind all this, he says to God. 'I trust in your unfailing love.' In my trials, he says, I find all this goodness and love, eternally strong and sure.

So the next time Luck surprises you with bad news or Fate overwhelms you with it, fear not. Your universe may be collapsing but the universe is only temporary. Fate and Luck belong to this provisional universe, and they will pass. Christ's salvation is primarily designed for universes and worlds that will never wear out. We will still be feasting there when those doomed wretches Luck and Fate are distant memories from another age.

ON HEROES

About how you just can't get them or be them
(2006)

This is about hero-worship, something that perhaps is a temptation to all of us, especially when we are new to the faith and rather vulnerable.

You just can't get the heroes these days. In previous eras of church history, the world seemed to be full of clean-limbed individuals who lived hard-working and praiseworthy lives while preaching the gospel, shutting the mouths of lions and being sawn in two, often all at once.

Today we live in a world where even the best of us are seen as badly flawed. And even those squeaky-clean saints of former years have been re-graded. No decent biography or obituary is complete these days without a listing, tactful or otherwise, of a few of the subject's faults and misdemeanours.

Like a photo culled from the web and then enlarged, heroes don't seem to have that fine-grained resolution that means their lives look good on billboards.

To take just one example, the pioneering founder of the Salvation Army, William Booth, fearless fighter for the poor and needy, once got so mad with his children that he took a gun and shot the family dog. When he realized how upset they were, he had it stuffed and brought back into the house. Then he got mad again because they didn't thank him. He was one of many leaders down to the present time who were perhaps better pioneers than they

The sandwich

were parents. How many children of Christian heroes could tell stories of tyranny? Plenty.

It was also said of Booth that orders he gave were to be obeyed without question. However, if anyone tried to give orders to him, he was free to ignore them because he must obey God and not men. This is a handy tip for team-working that I expect you to file for later use.

It's better this way

Yet even in this cynical age, we Christians can still fall into the beguiling trap of hero worship. This is how it seems to work. We go along in the Christian life like Goldilocks, finding some things too hot for us, and other things too cold; some things too wild, other things too tame. Then we stumble upon someone who just seems to have everything just right. We like what they say or write. Or we like their churches, or their leadership. It's such a relief to find them. These people seem to embody just what we aspire to in Christian living. What heroes they are. We start collecting CDs of their sermons and buying their books.

The apostle Paul found plenty of hero-worship when he listened to a report about the church he planted in Corinth. Some people thought he, Paul, was everything you could wish for in an apostle. Others preferred the eloquent and powerful speaker Apollos. Still others spoke fondly of Peter, who of course had worked with Jesus for three years, was presumably a fund of colourful stories, and of whom Jesus had said, 'on this rock I will build my church.'

On heroes

Paul wouldn't have any of it. I think he found hero-worship, at its root, a sign of not-being-properly-grown-up. He told the Corinthians, *we are all your servants*.

So two things: your hero isn't perfect, and he will let you down. And those other guys who you already know aren't perfect, and who you think don't quite get it right, maybe they have things to say into your life after all. By extension this is true of denominations and movements too. All kinds of Christian writers on the bookshelf can bless you. Bible-Presbyterians and charismatics can both feed your soul. In my view.

You're the ones in charge of your lives, concludes Paul. Don't follow people or movements blindly or totally. Weigh things. Take responsibility. Be your own person before God.

That's a sample of what Paul was always saying to new Christians, of course: don't be faddish, don't be blown off course, don't be a slave to the latest trends, be deeply rooted in God for yourself.

Remember their faith

There is another side to this, though. Let's not be hero-worshippers. But let's not cut everyone and everything down to our puny size either.

When the writer of the letter to the Hebrews wanted to stiffen the spines of the people he was writing to he reminded them of the saints of the past. He didn't claim they were perfect, or that we should model our lives on theirs exactly. He didn't set them forth as an example of how it should be done, in the good old days, when saints were real saints. But he did say, 'consider their faith'.

The sandwich

They weren't perfect, but they stuck it out. They failed, their hearts failed sometimes, it was difficult – the Bible is full of their failings -- but they stuck it out.

Paul says the same to Timothy, almost his last written words, eloquent as ever: 'You, however, know all about my teaching, my way of life, my purpose, faith, patience, love, endurance, persecutions, sufferings ...' (2 Tim 3:10-11)

And then he says,

'Continue in what you have learned.' Stick it out like I did. Do better than me, learn from my mistakes, do things differently, but stick it out. Keep the faith.

It comes to this

In summary, then, how do we treat Christian heroes? Well, don't build your life on them. Take what they have to give. And remember their faith.

You wouldn't want to do things exactly the way William Booth did. He got a lot wrong. But the poor lined the streets for his funeral. His children followed him into ministry. The organization he founded still bears fruit generations later. He kept the faith. A (flawed) hero. Just like you.

HEARING WRONGLY FROM GOD

About how putting your hands over your ears may impair your hearing
(2007)

This was sparked by Impact's *enjoyable habit of taking a quirky approach to an important truth and watching what happens.*

Hearing wrongly from God is easy and you hardly need any advice on it at all. Never mind that he is the Almighty and you are a half-pint. Never mind that he is bright-eyed with revelation, holding together the universe with his understanding, eager to breathe gentle words into your heart. You can hide from him, really you can.

Most people can be up and running, misunderstanding God consistently, in a matter of a few minutes. It's harder for children, of course. But anyone from teenage years upwards can master one of the few simple techniques that I'm going to tell you about. With regular practice, these become as easy as breathing. Don't believe the sceptics: you -- yes, you -- can insulate yourself totally against the Burning One, freeing yourself to worship what you truly love: your Blessed Self.

Here's how you do it.

1 Never surrender

This is the key to the whole thing. Remember Churchill's advice to the boys of his old school during the Second World War: 'Gentlemen! Never give up! Never give up! Never, never, never give up!' Don't yield an inch.

The sandwich

Resist God and he will, eventually, shuffle off and go bothering someone else. He won't strive with you for ever. There is an end to it.

Of course, God is quite a subtle foe in these matters. He will try to sneak in. We live with yearnings and aches: to love; to share our lives with others; to know the mysterious Essence beyond ourselves. A sunset, a face, a smile, they can seem like windows to heaven. They are not. Get a grip. Don't yearn. Don't be thankful. Don't seek God (have some sense!). Don't think. Take yourself in hand. Fulfil some pressing bodily need, put the TV on, gorge on some chocolate, go shopping, do something earthly to shake off these heavenly yearnings. You'll soon be fine again.

Or sometimes God tries to speak when you're going through a hard time. Really, he has no scruples. In tough times -- he knows and you know -- that you are inclined to panic. Grown men have been known to pray in toilets. Our advice remains the same. Remember Churchill, and never give up. In times of trouble say to yourself, 'at least I'm not tempted to try religion! I'm not a weakling! I can handle this!' You can fend God off pretty well with this sort of routine.

It is a basic rule: those who humble themselves, who strip themselves of vain arguments, who wait in silence for him, who surrender themselves absolutely and finally to his will: it's those he goes for. The rest of us are pretty safe. Keep fighting and there's always hope for you.

Hearing wrongly from God

2 Mix and match

Of course, even if he can't get at your heart right away, God will still try to influence you. He does it by subverting your ideas of goodness. But don't worry, it's easily prevented.

You want to be a good person, of course. God wants you to be a good person too -- there's the danger.

The way to avoid any possible trap here is to maintain a steady focus. You don't want to be just any sort of good person. You want to be a good person on your own terms. You want to mix and match God's ideas about goodness with your own. Ours is a consumer society and so this a perfectly reasonable thing to do.

For example, keep an eye on trends. You want to be good, but not poor, austere, sacrificial, wholehearted. Certainly not dull. Racy good will do it; or edgy good; exciting, taking people's breath away, not goody-good. Sexy, stylish, funny, rich and fulfilled. Hot, not cold. Chilli, not muesli. Passionate, fascinating, unpredictable, slightly scary. So mix up all your desires indiscriminately with whatever you fancy you may be hearing from God and you'll be just fine. He won't get a word in at all.

3 Accept no feedback

A patient, humble, teachable spirit is a dangerous thing.

Our minds are neural networks. They get things right only after much feedback and reinforcement: that's as true for hearing from God as it is in learning how to write your name neatly. You try, you show it to an adult, they praise

The sandwich

you and correct you gently, and finally, after hundreds of iterations, you get it right.

So it is with Hearing From God. People who hear consistently from God mull things over. Impressions waft into their minds, they pray over them, compare them with scripture, think them through, ask trusted advisers, wait on God for more revelation. They keep bringing a thing to God until it somehow holds together, the neural network is programmed with the right pattern, and a quiet peace settles on their hearts.

Knowing this, you can quickly see how you can mishear God almost 100% of the time. Be impulsive. Follow your gut. Then, be stubborn. Snatch at things. Cultivate prejudices. Don't ask advice. Only allow your Bible study to reinforce what you already know. Think the same way you always have. Follow your tribe. Be unteachable: after all, you already know all you need to know. Don't give houseroom to uncertainty, perplexity, ambiguity, hesitancy, diffidence. Tell yourself, 'tentative' or 'provisional' or 'subject to revision' is just another way of saying 'weak'.

I hope that's all clear. To sum up: if you want to keep your life clear of God's kindly revelation:

Be proud!

Strain after all the good things in life!

Be wise in your own eyes!

And you'll be just fine.

UNFAIR COMPETITION?
How it's OK to have megachurches
(2008)

Singapore is a city-state, and a city with a clutch of large megachurches. In a megachurch you can be part of a worshipping crowd of thousands and experience a Christian version of the theatre and spectacle that enriches urban life. Yet with congregations carefully organized into small groups, large churches also ensure that isolated city-dwellers have a network of close Christian friends to live out the Christian life with. Singapore also has smaller churches, and so it's a good question which type, if any, is most to be preferred. Back in the UK after enjoying a large church and a wonderful small group in Singapore, we resumed back at our 'local'.

Let's read out the charge-sheet first:

Like a great vacuum cleaner, megachurches hoover up all the Christians from miles around, leaving all the smaller churches to struggle and decline. And this is a Bad Thing.

It's not an empty accusation. I worship in an 80-strong church in Cambridge in the UK. We've declined slowly during the last 15 years.

Ten minutes' walk away is a church that in the last few years has gone from 250 to around 750. Not a megachurch in Singaporean terms, perhaps, but big enough. And it's a fine church. It's made up largely of students and people in their twenties or thirties. Our church has almost no-one in their twenties or thirties. And the pattern is now established. If you were a young

The sandwich

Christian family settling down in our part of the city, where would you go?

In praise of the megachurch

I thank God for our local megachurch. Here are some of the reasons:

Numbers are good. 'Numbers aren't everything,' people say. That may be true. But we all secretly or openly like large numbers. On the first Day of Pentecost, 3,000 people became Christians. If it were only 300, or 30, or 3, it wouldn't be such a good story. The book of Revelation talks about the people in heaven as a 'great multitude, that no-one could count' (Rev. 7:9). I take a lot of comfort from that. I would take less comfort if it said, 'Not a very big multitude' or 'Just a select few, really' or 'More of mini-tude'. I can't help feeling God likes big numbers just as much as any of us. 'God so loved the world' … you don't get bigger than that.

Megachurches remind us that the Church is big. A friend of mine once had this idea: wouldn't it be fun for every Christian in Singapore to put a Christian sticker on the front of their mailbox. Instantly, we'd see that we have brothers and sisters in every apartment block. The megachurches, perhaps, are the next best thing. They remind us the Christian faith isn't a little thing in a corner.

Megachurches can be exciting. In a small church it's perhaps easy to get bogged down keeping everything running. I find something very spiritually invigorating about people streaming into a church, packing it to the roofs. Something's happening. It's wonderful.

The solution to all our problems

Megachurches promote excellence. There's a bit of a danger here in that I'm not exactly sure what kind of worship or preaching God sees as 'the best'. I suspect he isn't overwhelmed with wonder at virtuoso music or massed choirs or funky worship bands. But, still, megachurches encourage an excellence, not a sloppy mediocrity. Let's be outstanding. Let's be the best. That's not a bad ideal.

Small isn't necessarily beautiful

Further, surely, *some* churches remain small because they're doing things wrong. If a pastor is slack in his work, is it a surprise if God doesn't give him so many sheep? If a group of elders run the church for themselves rather than for outsiders, or if they turn stiff-necked when the Holy Spirit urges them to change, is it a surprise that a church remains small?

So praise God for the megachurches who offer an alternative and a challenge and a wide vision. At our local megachurch, they are not stealing sheep, but they are growing lovely green grass. That's a challenge to the rest.

Let's hear it for the small churches

But I've learnt to praise God for my small church too.

God is a God of variety. It is entirely like God to create churches of every possibly shape and size. We are not like Malaysian rubber trees, all clones of a single plant. The only way to bring the gospel to a diverse world is to have an exceedingly diverse range of churches. We can be sure that God loves, blesses and desires churches of all possible sizes to thrive.

The sandwich

Jesus is concerned to produce fruit in our lives, not fat. It seems to me the Christian life is best lived on the edge. We have hard work and struggles. We find his strength in our weakness, his riches in our poverty, his hope in our despair. In our church, our lack of young families has had many good effects on us. Not least, the church has developed ministries that attract the non-Christians around us. We have an unusual commitment to the poor and needy, because we have a lot of needy people in our congregation. Unlikely people get to take the lead at times, because there's no-one else. We would have missed some of this had we been bigger, more successful, more slick.

Innovation starts small. All the best ideas start small. Our church, un-hampered by being a successful 'brand' has started many ministry initiatives. In this we have unintentionally become part of a wider movement in the UK which is seeing youth churches, cafe churches and other fresh expressions of church springing up. Often these unorthodox Christian meetings include a meal. If you only ever want to be part of a congregation of 200 or 2000, rather than one of 20, you will miss a lot of the new fun, and a lot of the good food.

The outward appearance is nothing, the inward appearance everything. I'm learning that the New Testament is almost one long story describing how that-which-is-despised has a better handle on the kingdom of heaven than that-which-looks-great. From the first statement of 'blessed are you who are poor' to the first witness of the resurrection -- a woman who mistook the Risen Messiah for a gardener -- Jesus seems to delight in the non-great, in the ordinary, in the below average, in the poor. When I look around at the wrinkled, spotted, streaked and hairy faces of our ordinary

The solution to all our problems

congregation taking Holy Communion together, I feel God's pleasure.

The real lesson

I am slowly (and painfully) learning not to mind when people choose the local megachurch over our little congregation. (OK, I do still feel a little jealous. We could use some fresh pairs of hands.) But I've found such riches serving God in our church -- our church which sends out a bus in the morning to collect old people, rather than students; whose worship creaks sometimes; and which at times has hosted more mentally ill people and people with learning difficulties than bright, young middle-class families.

At the end of John's gospel, it's recorded how Jesus talked to Peter about the path Peter would follow, one that included martyrdom. Peter wanted to know what would happen to John, his rival. Jesus told him, in effect, 'mind your own business. You follow me.' (Read the story in John 21:15-21.)

When we ask about megachurches adversely affecting smaller churches, I think Jesus' answer would be much the same. Whatever type of congregation we belong to, Christ is Head of the whole Church; Lord of our lives; and much smarter than we are. He's bigger than these issues and he knows what's best. Either church can be his place of fruitfulness for us. 'You follow me.'

THE GOD THAT TRUSTS

About how being trusted feels just like being abandoned
   (2009)

I wrote this oblivious to the storm that was about to hit us, with heart problems leading to ambulance rides, hospital spells and near-death experiences in 2009, 2011 and 2013. Happily, God and my wife and I were still found all clinging to each other when those storms blew out.

Let me get a heretical thought out of my system first.

I was listening to the singer Katie Melua who had a modest hit in 2007 with a slightly wacky song called *If you were a sailboat*. There's a line in that song that goes like this:

You took a chance on loving me

I took a chance on loving you

Here's my heretical thought: *that's how it feels between us and God.*

Listen to your good and true church leaders

Of course our church leaders, if they are good and true church leaders, will tell us that thought is theological nonsense on all kinds of levels. Here are two:

1.*Loving and trusting God isn't a gamble.* God, our leaders might remind us, has a decent record of keeping his promises. He can hold onto everything we give to him. He has the most enormous handkerchief for all our tears.

The sandwich

He's not just good at faithfulness, he's the wellspring of it. Well, true.

2. God loving and trusting us isn't a gamble either. This is *God* we're talking about. God whose judgement might be said to be fairly sound. God who has a good idea how things will turn out in the end, because both the beginning of history and its end are familiar territory to him. When he set his love on humanity, when he offered the wide arms of Jesus to anyone who will rest himself in them, he wasn't messing about, calculating the angles, whistling in the wind, or vaguely hoping things will come good. He's going to finish what he started. When he sets his love on us he is most definitely *not* thinking:

You took a chance on loving me

I took a chance on loving you

But that's how it feels

Except that's how it feels, quite often.

Consider Joseph, patriarch, grand vizier of Egypt, and sometime irritating younger brother. His brothers sold him into slavery, doing something that many an elder brother has only dreamed of.

It set up one of the classic narratives of the Old Testament: 17-year-old Joseph trusted God. Ever-old, ever-young God trusted Joseph. Joseph is sold on to an Egyptian official but works hard and becomes a top employee. He refuses to sleep with his boss's wife but gets imprisoned for it anyway. He rises to a senior position in the prison and has hopes for people putting in a good word for him with Pharoah, but his hopes are dashed yet again.

The God that trusts

Still God and Joseph trust each other. Finally, of course, thanks to realizing that Pharoah's puzzling dream is actually a weather forecast[1], he is appointed Pharoah's No. 2 and the story ends happily. He trusted God. God trusted him. And it all worked out.

Consider Mary, mother of the Lord Jesus. I think she was a teenager too. (Only a teenager, surely, would believe such a madcap idea as the 'the power of the Most High will overshadow you. So the holy one to be born will be called the Son of God' (Luke 1:35). Sensible mothers clamp down on that sort of stuff.) We know that Mary found a friend in her cousin Elizabeth. She found another in her husband-to-be who stood with her through it all. But presumably Mary had a mother, and aunties, and a granny or two. What did they think of her? What did her neighbours whisper? What did Joseph's friends laugh about? How could Mary walk down the street in Nazareth as her bulge grew? Was she always the serene figure of mediaeval art? Not if she was a human being, she wasn't.

Surely the Patriarch Joseph and the Virgin Mary, as well as every other person who has ever loved and trusted God in dark places, went through times when they could sing:

You took a chance on loving me

I took a chance on loving you.

---

[1] As Tim Rice put it in *Joseph and the Amazing Technicolor Dreamcoat*, 'Noble King, there is no doubt / what your dream is all about/ all those things you saw in your pyjamas/ are a long-range forecast for your farmers'

The sandwich

We might wonder how *God* felt as he watched these dear servants cry their tears. I can't see God sitting smug and aloof: what kind of Father is that? Did God too, somehow, worry about them? Did He, as it were, sit on his hands, longing to help, determined not to, nervous of the outcome? Somewhere within his all-knowingness and his almightiness could he, too, have sung:

You took a chance on loving me

I took a chance on loving you

These are questions for high-ranking and deeply bearded theologians, of which I am not one. But I'd love to know how you can be a Father and *not* feel vulnerable when you watch your children hurt.

The power of powerlessness

The problem is this: *God trusting you feels exactly the same as God abandoning you.* That's trust. There can't be trust without a letting go. God backed Joseph to endure the disappointment, the self-doubt, and the injustice, and he did. God trusted Mary to endure the painful conversations and the laughter in the street, and she did.

So why does God put us, and perhaps himself, through all this pain of trusting? Here's why.

God wants sons (and daughters), not slaves. Being trusted makes you grow. Trust leads to trustworthiness. This world does not need more Pharisees, who trust the rule-book and recipe book, never think creatively, never cook something new. It does not need lazy miserable servants, scared that God is a taskmaster, who bury their gifts within a fear of failure, who never want to be vulnerable.

The God that trusts

This world needs people who are built up by the power of trust. Trusted, trustworthy people. Read Paul's first letter to Timothy (I'm paraphrasing): *I thank Christ Jesus our Lord, who has given me strength, that he considered me faithful, appointing me to his service ... this is a trustworthy saying ... entrust the church to trustworthy people ... Timothy, guard what has been entrusted to your care.*

Trustworthiness will see the Church through, Timothy.

And so it will. Through the infectious power of trust, God is raising sons and daughters, confident in his love and favour, sure of his power, creative and happy, free to innovate, free to fail, free to wonder and dream and love and fight and transform the world. The dreamer Joseph ran a country. The peasant Mary made the Incarnation work. But previous bold generations of saints haven't exhausted all the fun. There's still some left for us.

God trusts you. Go with it. It will hurt. But it's OK.

THE PRACTICAL CHALLENGES OF BEING AN ANGEL

About finding the right broom tree, virgin, apostle, or musical note
(2010)

For a Christmas issue, the team asked me to think about whether or not it was fun being an angel. I'm pretty sure it wasn't because they mistook me for one. Happily I was having great fun studying the English poet John Milton around the time and some of that spilled into this article.

Is it fun being an angel?

All we really know about angels is what the Bible tells us, and the Bible doesn't tell us very much.

Breakfast is served

One thing we never see, for example, is an angel making a mistake. Elijah is hungry, exhausted and depressed under a broom tree. Journeying (let us presume) from heaven, an angel locates the right country, the right desert, and even the right broom tree. Then he fills a jar of water, lights a fire, finds some flour and oil, bakes bread, and gives Elijah a gentle tap on the shoulder. The account in 1 Kings 19 doesn't say whether he also coughs politely and says, 'Room service' or 'Breakfast is served' but the care of the weary prophet could not be more tender. Angels are good at their jobs; the Bible doesn't say how they learn the skills.

Or take the angel that slips into the prison where Peter is sleeping, bound, you remember, by two chains between

The sandwich

two soldiers, in Acts 12. First he brings some light into the room. Then he gives Peter a poke, or possibly a kick. Presumably the angel has remembered to sedate the guards since it is hard to imagine the Apostle being woken without giving out a mighty snort or wondering loudly what is going on. The angel then looses the chains, helps Peter to dress, reminds him to take his cloak, dodges the sentries, and makes the iron prison door open all by itself. Peter emerges blinking in the moonlight. The angel leads him down a further street before vanishing. I can picture the Apostle Peter as one of these people who finds waking up a challenge. But eventually he realizes what has happened, his head clears, and he sets off for the house of Mary, the mother of John Mark, to bring an unexpected end to the church prayer meeting.

How do the angels do this?

Worship

Or take worship. Perhaps this is the main work of the angelic host. Angelic choirs celebrated the Creation: God in his answer to Job talks about the time when 'the morning stars sang together and all the angels shouted for joy' (Job 38:7). Angels celebrated the Incarnation, giving a bunch of shepherds and a flock or two of sheep the most extraordinary musical moments ever seen on earth (see Luke 2:9). And Revelation portrays angels helping bring about the birth of the new heavens and the new earth, rejoicing all the while. The beginning, the middle and the end of the world are all celebrated by major compositions and performances.

But we never know more than this. Who writes the music? Are there auditions for the best parts? Do these

On being an angel

choral occasions require weeks of practice, learning exactly when to come in with the next 'Worthy are you O Lord'? Are there arguments over musical style? Is Western classical style old hat or is Bach still composing up there?

Or take the complex and difficult issue of angels at war. In our age of rifles and rocket-propelled grenades, would angels still appear with drawn swords, as they did to Balaam and David? Who does the procurement for these weapons? Do the same suppliers also equip the bad angels?

The hobbies of bad angels

Perhaps the greatest writer to think about these questions was the seventeenth-century English Puritan, John Milton, in his epic poem *Paradise Lost* (which you can read, with helpful notes, on the internet).

Most of Milton's poem is about the bad angels, who, as many critics have observed, Milton seems to find more colourful than the good ones. In Book II, Satan heads off to try to precipitate the Fall of Man. The rest of the Satanic host occupy themselves in Hell until he gets back. Milton lists some of their hobbies while they wait:

1. *Hold an angelic Olympic games,* 'Upon the wing, or in swift Race'

2. *Practice the arts of war.* 'Armies rush/ To Battel in the Clouds'

The sandwich

3.　*Form a singing group*: 'Others more milde / Retreated in a silent valley, sing / With notes Angelical to many a Harp'

4.　*Argue* about 'Providence, Foreknowledge, Will and Fate,' like students at a Bible college and (also like students at a Bible college) 'found no end, in wandring Mazes lost.'

5.　*Explore*. Unfortunately, since it is Hell they are exploring, they only find, 'many a dark and drearie Vaile … and many a Region dolorous.'

The end of it

Enough speculation. It *might* be fun being an angel because of the occasional James-Bond-like assignment. It might be fun to have your lunch bought by some generously hospitable Christian who is unaware that his guests are angels at all (See Heb 13:2). It might be fun to compose some angelic music and have it performed in front of the Throne of God.

But what certainly *is* fun is hanging around God's throne and Christ's church. There are all these people coming to Christ every day, each one causing rejoicing among the angels in heaven (see Luke 15:10). Hebrews 12 talks about 'thousands upon thousands of angels in joyful assembly,' like a happy football crowd.

And there's worship of God himself. Some people wonder how worship can be all that enjoyable: some of us get tired of it after half an hour on earth. How will we feel after half a million years? How might it be for the angels?

On being an angel

Perhaps there are possible answer to this question. First, surely for both people and angels, being in God's presence isn't only about giving out: we are nurtured and nourished by God's presence like a tree in the sunshine. We don't just worship God, we bask, like reptiles in the heat. The glory of God is sunshine to the soul. I can bask in the sunshine of God's love, swim in its sea, for a long time. Perhaps the angels do too.

Second, there's variety. One of God's promises to us, the Church, is this:

... in the coming ages he ... [will] show the incomparable riches of his grace, expressed in his kindness to us in Christ Jesus. (Ephesians 2:7)

Notice how it says 'coming ages', not 'coming age'. The idea perhaps is age following age of seeing grace's 'incomparable riches', fresh epochs, leading to fresh discoveries.

Third, maybe we'll enjoy the present moment more intensely. The sadness of any sweet moment (for me anyway) is the thought that it will end. Every farewell, every passing season (for those of us who have seasons) is a foretaste of our future decay, the trickle of sand through our hour-glass. The burden of the passing of time is eased in eternity and we will be free to experience the now without worrying about the then.[2]

---

[2] I'm grateful to my friend Andrew Bowker for this suggestion.

The sandwich

So we don't know too much about how the angels operate. In truth, we know almost nothing. But seeing God at work in the church, as they do, and spending times wrapped up in the presence of God, as they surely are—it's *got* to be fun.

THE PRAYER MEETING

About how God wants us naked, but we keep reaching for our clothes.
(2011)

Around the time I was writing this article, my wife Cordelia's youth group was taking the lead in 24-7 prayer times in our church in the UK. Given the nocturnal preferences of teenagers, this meant a few groggy nights in prayer rooms, even though Cordelia is otherwise a person who likes her sleep.

The beauty of vulnerability

A quick survey of effective pray-ers in the Bible shows that there is something about naked vulnerability in prayer that is a sweet smell to God.

In the Old Testament the childless Hannah goes to the temple 'weeping bitterly' as she prayed to the Lord. In the New, a woman who can't stop bleeding pushes through the crowd to touch the edge of Jesus' cloak. Four men dig through the roof to present a paralysed man to Jesus. The distinguished synagogue ruler falls at Jesus' feet and begs him to come and heal his daughter.

Jesus told stories to encourage artless, single-minded asking. There is the man in Luke 11 who needs some bread from a friend. The friend is in bed. But the friend gets up and rustles up some loaves, not, says Jesus, because he's his friend, but because of the man's 'shameless audacity' in asking. A corrupt judge does the decent thing for a widow because she's wearing him out with her constant asking. The judge just wants her to shut up (see Luke 18).

The sandwich

It's hard to imagine how Jesus could urge us more strongly to sweet, single-minded, vulnerable asking. *Keep on asking*, Jesus says, *keep on seeking. Keep on knocking.* Make a nuisance of yourself in Heaven.

The love of clothes

Church prayer meetings, in my experience, can occasionally fall slightly short of this ideal. Finding ourselves in a room together before God for a whole hour or more, we start reaching for the protective clothing. We are happy to talk about God. We are happy to discuss problems with each other at length. We are even happy to talk to God in a general way, politely making suggestions for him to take up.

This is not altogether a bad thing. It's good to do Bible study, it's good to share problems, and there are many situations where it is our job to pray generally, rather than specifically. The Bible instructs us to pray, generally, for kings and all in authority, for example, that we may live quiet and peaceful lives in all godliness and holiness. (See 1 Timothy 2.)

But we are also called to world-changing, urgent, naked, single-issue praying. How can we build that into the church's prayer life? Here are a couple of suggestions.

Shake things up

Sometimes it helps just to shake things up. The 24-7 prayer movement has been a blessing to our little church (as to many others). Many churches have gone much further than we have, but here's how it has worked for us:

1. Announce a special week, or weekend, of prayer.

The prayer meeting

2. Put up a rota in the church dividing the weekend into hour-long slots.

3. Encourage as many people as possible to choose a slot.

4. Build a prayer room. As well as prayer information, furnish it with different ways for people to express themselves in prayer. For example, some may want to draw pictures. Others may enjoy a graffiti wall, where people can write up their prayer requests and feelings. We've had worship books and music available.

I remember vividly our church's first attempt at a week of 24-7 prayer. It was lovely arriving in the morning, waiting my turn outside the prayer room. When the person in the prayer room came out, we'd maybe exchange a quick greeting. But then it would be into the room and to work. The prayer room got slightly smelly over the week, the graffiti walls and journals filled, pictures were drawn. Not many of us were 'prayer warriors'. Many more of us were probably 'prayer worriers'. But people took their turns on the rota. I was proud of our little 100-member congregation stretching out beyond our comfortable places into the holy vulnerabilities of an hour alone with God.

Lead the meeting

Outside of special prayer emphasis times, it is certainly possible to spice up the regular, church or missionary prayer meeting. Some of the most notable prayer meetings in the Bible show us how.

The sandwich

One of the most moving prayer-sessions in the whole Bible is the story of King Jehoshaphat in 2 Chronicles 20. Faced with a great army ranged against him and owning not too many military assets of his own, the good King Jehoshaphat gathers his people. Listen to his prayer:

They are ... coming to drive us out of the possession you gave us as an inheritance. Our God, will you not judge them? For we have no power to face this vast army that is attacking us. We do not know what to do, but our eyes are on you. (2 Chronicles 20:11-12).

Or look at the Early Church, after Peter and John's first arrest. The church raised their voices together and prayed *'enable your servants to speak your word with great boldness. Stretch out your hand to heal and perform signs and wonders through the name of your holy servant Jesus'* (the full story is in Acts 4).

I count four ingredients in these prayer times that we can incorporate into our own meetings:

1. Take time to remind people of truths and promises of God.

2. Outline the situation you face.

3. Pray specifically, urgently, for a specific thing or things to happen. This is where we step from comfortable prayers into uncomfortable ones. We are praying for the specific, not the general.

4 Keep praying for those specifics until an answer comes.

The prayer meeting

In Jehoshaphat's time, the prayer meeting ended when the Holy Spirit stirred someone to give a prophecy. In the session in the Early Church, the room shook. In our prayer meetings it can be as simple as a sense of urgent intercession being replaced with an atmosphere of peace and praise. We asked, God answered, it's over. We don't need to pray any more, because we asked the Lord for a specific thing and now we have peace that he has heard us.

This doesn't happen at every meeting. It didn't happen all that much in the Old Testament or the Early Church. But it can still happen. The church's prayer life needs to have a routine but it doesn't need to *be* routine. Variety, good leadership, and an honest, naked, vulnerability before God can make it extraordinary. Let's go for it. As the former slave-trader John Newton— himself, miraculously converted— put it:

Thou art coming to a King

Large petitions with thee bring.

THE EMPTY NEST

The hole truth
(2013)

Before I wrote this, Cordelia and I went to a seminar on transitions, hosted by an English speaker named Maureen Stringer. Some of this material, perhaps filtered through me, originated in that excellent seminar and is due to her. This article also roughly coincided with a season that saw our kids who not so long ago had been pedalling toy tractors or carrying dolls by the hair, breaking our hearts by growing up and going to University (not necessarily in that order). But we mended.

A principle for life

When something drastic happens, you need something to hold onto.

I walked my daughter down the aisle last August and we installed my son at University for his second year in October. Given that my wife and I haven't changed home, career or spouse in 20 years, nor suffered a major bereavement, I think we've had few more drastic changes in our normally-placid lives than our two offspring leaving home. (I suppose their arrival -- one 17 days late in England, the other 20 months later, on time, in Singapore -- would count as more disruptive, but that was a long time ago.)

Fortunately there is something to hold onto.

'Seek first the Kingdom and his righteousness' is a principle we can live by all our life.

The sandwich

We can work out what it means for us first as schoolchildren, perhaps, then as singles, then as young married couples. Then we're in our thirties maybe and all our time is taken with work, family, church, a glorious couple of decades that some people find flies past too fast. Still we can use that golden principle to set our course.

And then the children are gone: perhaps in a shower of confetti, perhaps on a plane to a university in the West. Empty nesting can feel like the end. No longer is our family together under one roof. The bundles of humanity that we carried home from hospital and for the next two decades fed, cleaned, taught, worried about and hugged have left the building, and perhaps taken some of our identity and meaning with them. Who are we now? What are we for? What, in the end, is the use of an empty nest? Isn't it, by definition, past its usefulness? By implication, aren't we?

It's time to revisit that calling yet again. 'Seek first his kingdom and his righteousness.' Like a spacecraft getting a gravity boost by whizzing close to the Sun before heading to the outer solar system, so we empty nesters can take in a fresh burst of healing sunshine and feel a fresh impulse of energy for the next stage in our journey.

Fresh ingredients in the soup

And it's different this time. We may be better off financially than ever before. We may have a better sense of who we are and what we are good at. So we have some fresh ingredients to throw into the pot as we 'Seek first his kingdom and his righteousness' as empty nesters:

The Empty Nest

Gratitude. Hey, we made it this far. Enough of our contemporaries have succumbed to cancer or heart attacks; enough of them, perhaps, still struggle uncomfortably uphill, cumbered by difficult marriages or handicaps of all kinds.

For whatever reason, by the grace of God, we are still standing. We belong to a generation that may be taking pills to keep us well, but we are not worn down by the afflictions that took down better men and women than us in previous days. The Protestant reformer Martin Luther (it could be said) won victories against the Pope, the Devil, the whole medieval religious structure and perhaps even inaugurated the modern world. But on balance he probably lost the battle in mid-life against gout and indigestion. That is probably not our fate and it is a gift of God.

Expect, and enjoy, a wintertime in the soul. The kids leaving home can feel like a wintertime descending on our soul. Transitions, whether they are expected (like the empty nest) or unexpected (like a bereavement) follow a pattern: a loss, a winter-time, a fresh start.

Winter is a normal part of the life of the soul. And it can't be rushed or avoided. Living as I do in the Northern Hemisphere, I could (wonderful thought) avoid the English winter every year by living in Singapore between January and March. But in our own souls we can't migrate to the tropics. Nor should we try. The winter-time is frustrating. It might feel like nothing is happening, but under the ground, roots are being pushed down, everything is being readied for a new start. We are internally re-orienting ourselves for a new day. So we need

The sandwich

to recognize what is happening and be gentle with ourselves through the winter of a transition:

- Remember we may be stressed, and perhaps give ourselves and our loved ones some leeway.

- Take time alone with God. It doesn't have to be a time crammed with prayer requests for others. We can just worship, wait, *be* in God's presence. And we can revisit some of God's promises. What are my 'sealed orders' from God? What has he laid on my heart to do? Someone said, 'don't die with your music still inside you'. In this wintertime we can ask God about this. What would I truly regret not doing if I got to the end of my life and hadn't done it?

- Find a friend to walk and talk with us through this winter walk.

- Take time to de-clutter our life. Perhaps now would be a good moment to throw away our notes from university, even if we're just replacing them in storage with our kids' notes. Let's give away some of our possessions. Better days are coming and we want our lives to be as lean and fit as they can be.

- Keep waiting. The wintertime will end in its own sweet time. Some transitions take years. That's OK.

- Live each day at a time. Wintertime isn't without its compensations. Brighter, busier days will return, but it won't hurt us to have a quiet season, reflecting, perhaps reading, talking things through, spending time with God, waiting.

The Empty Nest

Celebration. Disorienting and perhaps sad the empty nest may be, but we have reasons to celebrate too. Here are three:

1. *We did it!* The empty nest is an achievement. We've raised kids! We've changed nappies, helped with homework, found lost soccer kits, spent time with them (or not) imparted wisdom (such as it is), told them the same jokes (many times). Whether we were a good or a bad parent, or whether we hurt or helped our children (probably both), it's mostly over now. But we put in a shift. We may have regrets, but we probably did OK. And we have a stash of wonderful memories that no-one can take away, and so do our kids.

2. *Comfortably worn.* Along the way, raising kids changed us. When we are young, we learn to rely God's faithfulness or goodness because the Bible promised them to us. But when we're older, we can rely on these things because we've proved them. We know them because we've lived them. Our lives, like much-loved shoes, have become comfortably worn, not stiff; and good for many more miles.

3. *Time.* Maybe until now it may have been partially true that we haven't had enough time. We have had kids around who could call on our time at any time. Like broken cars or leaky plumbing, they need maintenance on their terms, not on ours. But that excuse (if it was an excuse) is now just an empty bedroom in our apartment.

Many of us wistfully think of a day coming when 'If only I had time, I would...' Well, now we have the time. It may not feel like it; it may not just fall into our laps. But

The sandwich

it is there. We have the time to learn the piano, or volunteer at church, or spend a year reading great novels, or complete that MA. If we don't take the opportunity now, we probably never will.

The principle revisited

One day soon, our souls will wake up from its wintertime slumber caused by the loss of our kids. We will be ready for a new start. At that wonderful stage in our lives we can seek God's Kingdom with a breadth and depth we've never known before. This is how to cope with the empty nest, not to see it as a loss to recover from but as a kind of base camp in the mountains from which to climb further. Let's:

1. *Run to win*. Better yet, *run your own race*. Athletes learn whether they are designed for the sprint or the 10k. We can learn our best pace, gifts and rhythms. We can focus. We can be harnessed to the right yoke and we can not only run to win but run the right race at the right pace. Running to win, now, seeking first the kingdom, for us can mean a blend of good rest and focused activity.

2. *Invest*. We should have an investment mentality. We've never been in a better place to invest ourselves in the Kingdom of God. Whatever our chosen sphere, let's build like the apostle Paul aspired to, on the foundation of Christ, with gold, silver, costly stones (see 1 Corinthians 3:11-14). Let's lay down the best of all we are for him. Let's invest in other people, helping their agendas and programmes. Let's nurture them as they struggle with things that we ourselves have struggled with. We know what it is to be just married, or to have a child that won't stop crying, or to wonder how we're going to fit everything

into a day. We can help carry some of these burdens for others.

3. *Major on what we're good at*. At the same time, we know, or should know by now, (in the words of the theologian Frederick Buechner) 'the place where your deep gladness and the world's deep hunger meet.' We have found our place to serve. That's not to say that at the empty nest stage we don't have time to serve others, help out, fill in gaps. But let's keep the main thing the main thing. The apostle Paul's most fruitful church-planting time was his mid-fifties. We too can find ourselves suddenly in the midst of our best work. At the core of many organizations, if you scratch deeply enough, are clusters of people in their fifties, active, experienced, fully engaged, holding it all together. Never before have we been so experienced, and so free.

4. *Give ourselves permission to be creative, to create beauty*. Finally, we can take time for beauty and creativity. This is true at all stages in life, perhaps, but never more so than when we are empty nesters. God's chosen replacement for ashes is beauty (see Isaiah 61:3). We can honour him and pre-figure his kingdom by creating beautiful things in his name. Looking at three empty nesters I know, I see one who has cut back his teaching schedule so that he can spend more time painting. Another has started growing her own food. A third works in software by day but by night builds things with wood or makes intricate, beautiful paper models. All of them are re-digging deep wells of creativity that God put in their hearts, and that perhaps got blocked in the child-rearing years. Now is the time to let the waters flow again.

The sandwich

The last word

A debate about abortion was rippling through the letters page of a national newspaper here in the UK. When exactly does life begin? At conception? When the foetal nervous system and brain develops? After 24 weeks' gestation? 'None of those' wrote in someone else. 'Life begins when the kids leave home and the dog dies.'

THE BIGGEST FAILURE IN THE BIBLE

How it happened
 (2014)

It was typical of editor Andrew Goh's quirky creativity to set me the question, 'Who's the biggest failure in the Bible?' I couldn't resist having a go.

To be the biggest failure in the Bible you must have a shot at being one of its greatest successes. This rules out a lot of people, such as Trophimus the Ephesian. In just three verses, this unheralded nuisance manages to (a) be the reason for the major riot in Jerusalem that put the apostle Paul in prison and (b) to fall sick in Miletus and not to be healed by that same great Apostle.

Trophimus, in other words, is that church member who means well but is surrounded with a zone of chaos and destruction wherever he goes. Possibly you know a Trophimus. But despite his high failure coefficient he is only a minor player in the grand story of redemption, so we strike him off our list. We might rule out Judas Iscariot for similar reasons. No-one in the whole Bible got it more wrong. The frightful verdict on his life, courtesy of Jesus himself, is 'it would be better for him if he had not been born' (Mark 14:21). That's certainly failure enough. May it never be said of us.

But Judas was only one of twelve apostles, and he was quickly replaced. The story went on without him. Let's also give the Old Testament figure Samson the push. Samson was the prototype charismatic-leader-traffic-accident-waiting-to-happen, impressive gifts,

The sandwich

unimpressive integrity. His life came literally crashing down but, still, Samson was a single judge, one of many in Israel, in a time when many were mucking things up. A sad example of a malfunctioning leader, yet not the Bible's greatest failure.

Instead let's try someone who could have been one of the leading figures in the whole history of redemption, a major player, who yet fell almost as far as it is possible to go. Our vote goes to Saul, first king of Israel.

'Hapless'

The word 'hapless' could have been invented for Saul. The *Oxford English Dictionary* defines Hapless thus: 'destitute of or lacking good fortune; unfortunate, unlucky. Hence also in later use: incompetent, clumsy.' There is just something doomed about Saul. It's made all the worse by his undoubted courage, good looks, and earnest efforts. Saul was a trier and had enough talent and potential to crash and burn while others had barely enough qualities to get off the runway.

Part of his haplessness was his capacity for public relations disasters. Saul strides onto the pages of the Bible not like David, fighting Goliath, nor like the Apostle Paul, helping kill the first Christian martyr (which at least demonstrated potential and commitment, albeit needing a little re-direction). No, Saul makes his entrance searching for donkeys, at which it is hard to look good. People who are looking for things are very irritating to people who are not looking for things, especially perhaps when those things are really big and furry and obviously not there.

The biggest failure in the Bible

Does Saul then redeem himself by demonstrating astonishing skills in tracking? He does not. Instead, it's recorded that his dad started to worry about him, which since Saul was a tall and scary grown man, and only perhaps 20 miles from home, is again not a massive vote of confidence.

It's left to Saul's servant to suggest they visit the prophet Samuel whose prophetic gifts may stretch to donkey-location services. Saul agrees, but, predictably, doesn't have any money. Perhaps he left his credit cards at home, another winning trait in a would-be leader. The servant stumps up the cash, and, so far, looks a far better person for a crisis than Saul himself.

Saul the hero

Yet despite the inauspicious start, Saul becomes king and does well for a time, against very difficult odds. Israel was overrun with the Philistines, who had a properly organized standing army, unlike Israel. The Philistines had the technological mastery, controlling all the iron manufacture. Coming from the smallest tribe, Saul lacked a power base. Worse, he also had to combat the prophet Samuel who was grumpy about the whole idea of Israel having a king. They had not had one before. Samuel, it seemed, was only allowing it because God had told him to, not because he personally thought it was a good idea.

You didn't mess with Samuel, he could summon earthquakes with prayer, but like many leaders he had a bit of a blind spot when it came to his own family. At the time of Saul's election, Samuel's sons were running the country -- badly. So there was a ticklish issue for a new king's in-tray. The old leader's sons aren't up to the job,

The sandwich

political reform is needed, but the decrepit old boy in charge can't face the facts.

Yet Saul made a good fist of being king. He rescued the threatened city of Jabesh Gilead by personally calling and leading an army. Aided by his son Jonathan, he inflicted spectacular damage on the Philistines against fierce odds. He fought off other raiders, surrounded himself with good people, declined to be vindictive against his political enemies, and was personally modest in his kingly lifestyle.

Samuel went into retirement and no more was heard of his sons. Saul knew, if he obeyed God, his kingdom could last forever. We have to believe that it was at least conceivable that Saul could have been what David later became-- the first king in a glorious, eternal line.

Yet it all fell apart. The honest, modest king morphed into a depressed, paranoid monster. He resorted to using a medium -- I think the only godly leader in the whole Bible who has sunk to consulting the spirits of the dead. And then he, his sons and his armourbearer all died in a decisive battle against the resurgent Philistines that set Israel's cause back for a long time.

Saul's fall

Saul got little credit for the good stuff but instead faced the full wrath of Samuel when he made two judgement calls in extremely pressed circumstances. It is, perhaps, another sign of the hapless: you get your appraisal done when you are having an extremely bad day. First, Samuel had told Saul to go to a mustering ground called Gilgal before a battle with the Philistines

The biggest failure in the Bible

and wait seven days until Samuel arrived. Saul had done as asked, watching while the Philistine forces multiplied around them. Saul's own army, just six hundred strong, was starting to desert. The seven days passed. The forthcoming battle looked terrible. Rather than wait any longer for Samuel, Saul himself made sacrifices to God -- and then Samuel turned up and condemned him. Samuel didn't apologize. Paraphrasing Tolkien's Gandalf the Grey, Samuel might have said, 'Late? A prophet is never late!'

The second time, Samuel ordered Saul to kill and destroy every living thing among the Amalekites, men, women, children, cattle -- a brutal, rare and difficult ask for the king. Saul's army did not seem overly troubled by hacking the heads off babies or slicing open pregnant women (this was a ruthless era), but they did object to seeing all that juicy beef going up in smoke uneaten. Steak won out over submission, and Saul didn't stop his army's ox-roast, and Samuel condemned him again, and removed his blessing.

You can say this is all a bit unfair. Saul was attempting to show leadership in terrible times. Things were going wrong all around him. Bloodshed was not far off. Who, in a war, gets all the decisions right? Desperate days require brave decisions. What would you do if your army was falling apart while you waited for a prophet to show up? How well would you fare when your hungry men wanted a well-earned barbecue and you were the only one blocking the way?

Anyway, didn't other leaders in the Bible commit worse sins than Saul and not get deblessed, as Saul was?

The sandwich

Abraham took things into his own hands when he fathered Ishmael rather than wait for Isaac. King David committed both murder and adultery. When in danger of their lives, the apostle Peter denied Jesus three times. Other apostles found they had urgent appointments elsewhere. Saul, by way of refreshing change, hardly ducked a fight in his life.

Saul's problem

So how did he end up as the Bible's biggest failure? First we note that it's in the times of deepest stress that we reveal who we really are. It honestly isn't all that hard to seem to be living a godly life when the seas are calm and the skies are blue. Only stress shows our true colours. So we shouldn't be surprised that it took difficult days to expose Saul's heart.

Second, God is God and he has the right to deal with disobedience in his servants differently. Abraham took matters into his own hands. So did Saul. Different circumstances and capacities were on show, but it was the same sin at its root. So perhaps in a sense the Bible is harsh on Saul, or at least gentle on Abraham. May God be gentle on us too!

Yet, third, Saul's fatal error really was a fatal error, and it set him apart in my view from Abraham and David and the apostles. Running through his life was a tendency, which wasn't a technical mishap, or a minor misjudgement; it was, finally, a misunderstanding of everything important about how God and people relate. Saul's regular mistake was to think God wants us to sort things out for ourselves, cope as best we can. Saul was talented enough to make this work for a time. But that isn't what God wants.   God wants us to trust him with our lives.

At Gilgal, the sacrifices honestly didn't matter; trusting God did. So your army's deserting while Samuel shows every sign of being caught in the traffic around Jericho? Trust God anyway. So your hungry army is mutinously eyeing up some fatted calves? Stand in their way. Trust and obey God. See if they'll really kill a king, or, muttering darkly, obey God after all.

Flawed like Saul

Haplessness haunted Saul. Worse, he then let jealousy gnaw at him unchecked and as an older man became paranoid and vindictive. But the truth is we are all like that. We are all flawed like Saul, fatally flawed, each in our own way. Saul's real problem was not that he was fatally flawed, but that he didn't throw his fatally flawed self on the mercies and adequacies of God.

His real failure was a failure simply to trust and obey: 'Samuel said. "You have not kept the command the Lord your God gave you; if you had, he would have established your kingdom over Israel for all time"' (1 Sam 13:13), and 'Saul died because he was unfaithful to the Lord; he did not keep the word of the Lord and even consulted a medium for guidance, and did not enquire of the Lord. So the Lord put him to death and turned the kingdom over to David son of Jesse' (1 Chron 10:13-14).

I feel for Saul. I think he was a put in a job too difficult for him, and certainly at first he tried his best to make it work, earnest, brave, modest, sincere. The problem was, that isn't how it works between people and God. We are

The sandwich

all in roles too difficult for us. We all have impossible jobs. 'Whoever claims to live in him must live as Jesus did' says the first letter of John (1 John 2:6) How possible is that? It isn't.

The people who please God fall into the arms of the One who justifies the ungodly and the hapless and the useless. Through faith people conquer kingdoms. Through faith they live and die bravely. Through nakedly trusting God they take on armies. Through simple, trusting obedience they cheerfully face down the impossible. Better to die trusting God, they argue, rightly, than live relying on ourselves.

What can we learn from the Bible's biggest failure? Don't have fatal character weaknesses? No--we all do. Trust God with all your heart. Follow his commands rather than your own wisdom. Trust him unto death. Quite a lesson.

PRAYING FOR MIRACLES
About the sun rising again
   (2015)

The question I was set for this article was: 'How do we know when to stop asking and simply accept? What's the difference between surrender and giving up hope?'

We are treading on a tender spot here. Because we all know people who have been struck down inside a good healthy life. Some dreadful disease snaffles them and everything inside of us cries out, 'No! This is wrong.' So we pray for healing.

Worse (in a sense), we know that God *is* a healing God. In the person of Christ he walked on the earth and did not view suffering with a Roman stoicism or a Jewish shrug. He wept over it, climbed into the problems, and healed. The lame walking, the blind seeing, the deaf hearing, the dead being raised are signs of his Kingdom. These are the gifts he scatters as he walks among us. Jesus our King is full of compassion, fully engaged, and mighty to heal and save. Sin, evil, suffering, demons, death: he detests them all and went to the cross to purge all of them out of his lovely Universe.

We all know what is coming next: *yet so many are not healed.* I would be very surprised if in the circle of people you know and care about, there are not some for whom you are praying but who are not getting better. Others stay sick and in pain for a long time. What do we do? How do we pray?

The sandwich

***

I joined a community choir recently. I am a musical illiterate, but I am learning that some songs include a key-change. You are singing along happily enough, you think you're getting the hang of this, but then the composer introduces a key-change and often it takes the song to a whole new level. For example, the South African National Anthem includes five languages and a key change, because Nelson Mandela wanted to incorporate both the African National Congress anthem and the old white South Africa anthem, and five of South Africa's eleven languages, into one song. It makes the total experience a powerful statement of unity in a divided land. Without the key-change, it only would be half a song.

As we pray on for the unhealed, we must listen for God's key-change. Most of us who fall sick only want one thing: to get back to how we were. But with very many sicknesses and afflictions—cancer, surely--there is no going back. There is only going forward. Hence the need for the key-change. We just want to go home, but God is changing the landscape around us. In his terrible love, God is taking the evil and forging something good in us. This is why I suggest we let God lift our juvenile, confused, panicking prayers to another level. Of course it is not our prayers he is taking to another level: it is we ourselves. Then the song will be complete in us.

Here are some of the elements, so it seems to me, of God's key-change.

Praying for miracles

1. *Mystery.* In the gospels Jesus walked through a large collection of sick people at the pool of Bethesda and healed just one person (John 5:2-9). He stood in a cemetery full of dead people and called just Lazarus back to life (John 11:38-44). He must have seen a number of funeral processions but he interrupted only one, that of the widow of Nain's son (Luke 7:11-15). Why should some be singled out for instant healing and others not? It does not seem fair, nor can we explain why. It is a mystery. Mystery is like a cloud passing between us and the certainty of the living, loving Christ. We know the Lord is still there, but for the moment all we can see is the cloud.

2. *Eternity.* I guarantee you have nothing wrong with you that the resurrection will not put right. When a person passes from this land of the dying to the land of the living with peace on their face, bags packed, ready for eternity, surely that's a healing, that's the great healing, even if for us who are left it is a separation and loss. And even if the timing feels all wrong. So real, full healing is guaranteed for all who come to Christ, in eternity.

3. *The present moment.* Sometimes in our panic and fear we forget the importance of the present moment. Yes, let us ask God that a person's dreadful illness is totally healed. But let us not forget the *now*. 'God', we can pray, 'turn their anxiety into peace today. Make their soul happy today. Set a table for them in the midst of their enemies today.' In my limited experience of these

The sandwich

things, a visit, a word, something, can make your heart almost burst with joy, even if you are lying paralysed in bed and connected to quite a lot of tubes. People might argue that that's not the same as a proper healing. I am not so sure. It certainly feels pretty good at the time.

4. *Seeing what the Father is doing.* Someone once told me, prayer is not forcing God's arm; it is taking what is offered in his hand. Somehow we need to walk with the Holy Spirit through the winding paths of prayer and let him guide our prayers so that as we pray, we feel full of peace and confidence. If we feel led to pray for a glorious sunset to a good life, so be it. If it means praying the person with ulcers will feel secure in God so that he doesn't have to be a workaholic, that's fine too. I'm not a fan *at all* of sharing these insights with the patient; they have enough to cope with. I would suggest asking for God's leading, but then keeping the leading for your own domestic use.

5. *A meeting.* Some scriptures teach that everyone who came to Christ for healing *was* healed. See Mark 6:56, for example: 'wherever he went—into villages, towns or countryside—they placed the sick in the market-places. They begged him to let them touch even the edge of his cloak, and all who touched it were healed.' I believe these scriptures. Yet many today do not experience instant physical healing. How do we square this circle? Here's how it works for me. I believe that everyone I might pray for can and should meet

Praying for miracles

God. When the person meets God, in a sense, I can leave the two of them to it. The healing has begun. What goes on between them—instant healing; a long process of healing; abundant life amid continuing physical infirmity; healing fulfilled in eternity; or anything else—is between that person and God. Meeting God is the first and main thing. The core of healing is not getting physically better for a season until something else strikes us down. It's meeting Jesus. I think I can pray for any sick person that they will meet Christ, they will touch the edge of his robe, and the healing will begin. I use that prayer a lot and I really like it.

6. *The glory.* Hospitals, and let us be honest, sometimes a group of pray-ers, can make the patient feel like little more than a useless lump of meat. The sick person themself can start to believe that. But a sick person is not someone who has been suddenly shunted from a fruitful life to a non-fruitful one. He or she is not out of work, certainly not out of God's work. They may not be on the path they would choose, but they are still on a path. They can glorify God. In the Old Testament Joseph named one of his children 'Ephraim' which apparently sounds like the Hebrew for 'twice fruitful' and he explained why. It was because 'God has made me fruitful in the land of my suffering' (Genesis 41:52). That's a mighty prayer to pray for a sick person. 'God make her fruitful in the land of her suffering.'

The sandwich

> Back to the question we were set: *How do we know when to stop asking and simply accept? What's the difference between surrender and giving up hope?*

I think I'm arguing that there's a third option between simply praying for physical healing and simply surrendering the person to God. I've called it God's key-change, and it's praying that respects mystery and eternity, treasures the present moment, tries to listen to God, believes that healing starts when people meet Christ, and asks for fruitfulness even in their place of suffering.

It's worth a try.

ON SOULMATES

About how they sound like a good idea
   (2015)

Cordelia and I are still married, now for more than 30 years, despite my many failures in the romance, husband, and father departments. Whether I am qualified to dish out advice to others, I am not so sure. But I sneaked this article into the collection anyway.

We might start with a definition. Here's the *Oxford English Dictionary*:

Soulmate: A person who shares a deep understanding or bond with another; esp. one ideally suited to another as a lover or spouse.

The *OED* finds the first English use of the word in the poet Samuel Taylor Coleridge, himself a maker of an unhappy marriage. He is warning a young lady against a bad move in the marriage business and insists:

You must have a Soul-mate as well as a House or a Yoke-mate.

First recorded in 1822, the word didn't catch on at first. But then in the 1980s, its frequency in English writings began to soar and it continues to get more and more popular. (You can track this via Google's ngram viewer, which shows how words tumble in and out of use over the centuries.) I don't know that we can learn much from this, beyond that loose talk of 'soulmates' has become increasingly fashionable over the last generation.

The sandwich

But is it Biblical? Is it realistic? Is it an ideal or an idol? A holy thing or a Hollywood thing?

Holy or Hollywood?

We have to admit that within its pages, the Bible accommodates some rough-and-ready schemes for acquiring a life partner, and the whole soul-mate thing (falling in love, sighing, gazing at the moon, reciting poetry, that kind of stuff) is not, shall we say, the signature issue. Teenage girls enjoying a dance are abducted by a bunch of Benjaminites (see Judges 21). Women taken in war are washed, shaved, given new clothes, left for a month and then married by whomever captured them (Deuteronomy 21:10-14). A man could get off a rape charge by marrying his victim (Deuteronomy 22: 28-29). In these soils, you can imagine, it might take a while for soul-matiness to bloom.

But women-as-property was only ever one side of it, even in the Old Testament. Back then they knew all about love-marriages too. Think of Jacob, who had to work seven years as a dowry for his wife Rachel, but they 'seemed like only a few days to him because of his love for her' (Genesis 29:20). Or the book of Proverbs: 'May you rejoice in the wife of your youth ... may you ever be intoxicated with her love' (Proverbs 5:18-19). And Ecclesiastes, who sees love, and especially domestic love, lighting up and transforming the otherwise pointless-seeming hamster-wheel in which we spin each day. 'Enjoy life with your wife, whom you love, all the days of this meaningless life that God has given you under the sun' (Ecclesiastes 9:9).

The New Testament, of course, helped along the cultural shift from woman-as-property to woman-as-

On soulmates

companion. No wonder it was so popular with Greek women who finally found a faith that taught radical things like, 'Husbands, love your wives' (Ephesians 5:25) and 'Husbands ... be considerate as you live with your wives, and treat them with respect' (1 Peter 3:7). No wonder they embraced, taught and sometimes died defending Christian marriage.

The commonest New Testament understanding of how it is between a husband and wife is that they are 'one flesh', one interdependent whole. Where one is weak, the other might be strong. Where one is slow, the other is quick—and patient. Both see, feel, and decide things in different ways and on different priorities; together, though, they are a powerful whole. It's a picture of intimacy, communication, forbearance, trust, a shared load. Better yet, anyone who has hung around Christian churches for a while finds plenty of it lived out.

As we know, the New Testament even uses the picture of husband and wife to describe the relationship of Christ with his people. It's impossible to think of a higher compliment being paid to the idea of marriage. Does the Bible teach marriage should be intimate, open, nourishing, supportive, kind, and full of love? Er... yes.

So the human longing for a soulmate is one the New Testament seems to endorse. It has, and we should have, a high expectation of a good marriage. We can find a soulmate and love them for a lifetime. It's official.

More questions

That raises several more questions, especially if you are suffering something of a soulmate shortage.

The sandwich

For example: How do you know if you've a found a soulmate? More practically, do any of the current crop of potential soulmates look any good? What if you miss your chance? Is there such a thing as second best? Are you setting your expectations too high? Or too low? What to do if you have an awful feeling you have picked the wrong one?

I think we can attempt these questions in two ways. First, we locate them in a wider context: in the scary funfair of life, the ups and downs of acquiring a marriage partner are just another rollercoaster, subject to the same perils and (for the Christian) the same promises as all the other big things in life. Then, second, we grab hold of all the wisdom we can. Wisdom doesn't guarantee against failure or disaster; but it ensures we're still standing at the end, still loving God, having found a way through.

A rollercoaster, like all the others

First the context. We go hoping for love with insufficient data, little experience and conflicting advice and thoughts. Some of this we get from friends, some from novels, songs, plays, TV programmes and movies.

We are young and impulsive. It may be those parts of our brains that are good at caution haven't switched on yet. Or, in contrast, we may feel those parts keep setting off false alarms so often that we want to take the batteries out. Worse, we go looking for love in a world that is not just imperfect but actually broken, a place in part of selfishness, greed and betrayal. Worse still, some of the world's evil comes out of our own hearts and spills into our relationships. This is a world that can disappoint and hurt us, and in which we can harm others.

On soulmates

Acquiring a life-partner, in other words, is just the same as all the other big stuff: families, health, circumstances, careers. All these things can go well in our lives or badly. They can be a great blessing or things that trouble us every day. Or both. Through it all, though—this is the wonderful thing about following Christ—we walk hand in hand with a God who loves us and is good with broken things. 'Surely your goodness and love will follow me all the days of my life' (Psalm 23:6). 'I will never' says God of his people, 'stop doing good to them' (Jeremiah 32:40). These are promises to inspire even the most chicken-hearted among us to flap our wings and try to fly.

Investing in wisdom

Second, we grab hold of all the wisdom we can find. Here's a list. Some points are more personal, which I would not trust very far, others are Biblical, which I would trust very far indeed. Quite a lot are about steering a path between two opposite extremes.

1. Jesus did say, 'Seek first [God's] kingdom' (rather than running around after jobs, money or life-partners) 'and all these things will be given to you as well' (Matthew 6:33). Put God-stuff first and it will be fun to see who you bump into.

2. We don't need to panic about finding a soulmate. But equally, it doesn't do any harm to seek to meet new people in contexts you are comfortable with, which for a lot of us means the Internet.

3. Bible standards for relationships have stood the test of time. The older, crustier and grumpier I get the more I believe that Christians should only date Christians and that the old-fashioned idea of growing

The sandwich

in intimacy and keeping back the best stuff till you've formally committed your lives to each other, in public, in front of your mothers, is the best way forward. In the rest of life, we all know how good it is to serve time as an apprentice. Apprentices can make mistakes or even change careers before too much harm is done. Would you like a first-year medical student doing your heart transplant? Me neither. And there's something beautiful about two people learning love together, becoming vulnerable, making mistakes, growing in trust, an amateur love.

4. When you are considering a lifetime with someone, it is a massive decision so you may as well try to get it right. There is a fun way to do this. Do the friendship, the companionship, the growing intimacy. (OK, it's also potentially embarrassing and heartbreaking but the odd broken heart is perfectly normal and most people recover). It's essential to take time and get this decision as right as you humanly can. It isn't enough that the two of you have a shared passion for Manchester United or Star Trek. It means asking some plain questions, even deploying the brain and the critical faculties:

    1. Do I really, really like this person; or do they annoy or bore me a little bit?

    2. Am I a bit dazzled by the whole idea of having a boyfriend or girlfriend, of some physical intimacy, of the opportunity to look smug to my single friends?

    3. Are we compatible (age, education, culture, friends)?

On soulmates

    4. What do our families and friends think?

5. When you have doubts, face them, don't bury them. Talk about them with trusted friends. Do the doubts shrink or grow? That'll help you decide. I remember a friend who was a nurse and who secretly dreamed of marrying a doctor. Instead, a rough young farmer fell for her. My nurse friend pondered a long time but eventually saw beyond his slightly rustic manners and eating habits into his character and heart. She had to do a little rethinking, a little re-calibrating of her dreams, but really it was easy. Their forty or more happy years of marriage only ended with his death.

6. Eventually, go for it. Yes, it can go wrong in multiple ways. You can end up lonely and heartbroken. Take all the advice, think hard, pray hard, take your time, make up your mind, but then *do* something. I have watched too many men, content with job, home and girlfriend sit around doing nothing. And their girlfriends let them. Do something. Many cultures expect the man to do the asking. Ok, then guys, get on with it. You can do this. My proposal to my future wife would only earn one star in an Internet review. But at least I did it. And it worked. To the females I would say if he won't propose, break up with him and tell him that a very desirable person like you can't be left hanging around. Shock the little bozo into action.

And finally

    Three final points to put the quest for a soulmate in its proper place:

The sandwich

1. Every marriage, even the happiest, and some are very happy, sits somewhere on a scale of imperfection. Some people make bad marriages. They have a better chance of not doing so if they follow the advice given above, but it can happen anyway.

2. Our faith is designed for imperfection. Some people make bad or less than ideal marriages and still do OK by making the best of them and loyally loving. (I'm not referring to abusive or violent marriages: in that case, get out of there.) Some bad-looking marriages may actually be less unhappy than they appear. Some people cope with bad marriages the way others cope with long-term illnesses or difficult colleagues or family members or a myriad other life-changing disappointments and setbacks. It's sad but it's OK. Is there a place for divorce? Yes, but that's another subject. I know some who do take that step who later wish they hadn't.

3. Through Christ we inhabit a realm not just of love and faith (we commit to love people and trust God) but also of hope. In the final calculations, all the tears and disappointments of this life are just by way of painful stretching exercises prior to the energetic fun that is coming in eternity. In this life we might marry and be glad we did; or not marry and wish we had; or marry and wish we hadn't; or divorce; whatever; we did our best before God; and it's all prelude to the music to come. We truly have a Soulmate in Jesus. He is the proper locus for our longings and he won't disappoint us.

'GOD'S NOT FAIR'

About riding forth for justice on a very small horse
  (2016)

I am a younger brother, and my wife is a big sister to a younger brother, so we both have views on justice that were shaped early in life.

Ask anyone with a younger brother. Life is not fair.

We know that no two people are born equally favoured. We aren't given equal chances along the way. Here's the tip of the iceberg:

1. Younger brothers don't get told off; we do.
2. Some people blab on their phone all the time while driving and are never caught. Someone else uses the phone once, with the car stationary, in a family emergency, and has to pay a fine.
3. Babies born in Singapore can expect to live 83 years; others choose parents from Sierra Leone and may only average 50 years.
4. Wars are unjust and they happen randomly. My grandad was gassed, shelled and shot at as a teenager. My dad as a young man was merely shot at and shelled. I've never worn a uniform. My son has only done so as an out-of-school activity. What bad luck it was to have been born in an era of Hitler or Stalin.

Worse, in a sense: God, we believe, *is* fair. Nor does he think justice is merely an aspiration, a campaign promise, something to be put in place when he has sorted

The sandwich

out a few other things first. God *loves* justice (as Isaiah 61:8 says). He *does* justice: 'the Lord works righteousness and justice for all the oppressed' (Psalm 103:6). He *commands his people* to do justice: 'Do not pervert justice or show partiality ... Follow justice, and justice alone' (Deuteronomy 16:19-20).

God is just; life isn't. Yet God is all-powerful. So why isn't life fair? Below are a few thoughts.

We inhabit a wrinkle in eternity

We inhabit a wrinkle in eternity. It helps to realize this.

Eternity is forever--and it is filled with God and his kindness and fairness. Evil and suffering are temporary and are perhaps the equivalent of an attack of hiccups in this great grand goodness. In the big picture, all is thriving and bright. So far, so true. But let's zoom in on the wrinkle.

God is at work in history

God is working in the wrinkle. This is a central Christian teaching, and it is comforting but it doesn't make our question any easier. A God who set things up and then headed off for the evening, leaving us to it, would at least mean we could understand injustice. But that isn't an alternative the Bible offers. Instead, the Bible portrays God, like a master chef with hands in the baking bowl, up to his elbows in justice work every day. Here are some things he does:

God brings things to an end in his own time. This current world has mortality built in. People, cultures, empires

'God's not fair'

grow, ripen, rot. Everything passes. This is part of his architecture of history: extremely sad for those we love but rather helpful in the case of evil people and empires. If they lived forever, it would be a nightmare, Genghis Khan or someone would still be in charge. But in an evil world, universal mortality is almost a kind of mercy, certainly a way of capping off evil. 'A little while, and the wicked will be no more; though you look for them, they will not be found. But the meek will inherit the land and enjoy peace and prosperity' (Psalm 37:10-11).

God works on behalf of the needy. I once sat in the recovery area of an eye-surgery ward. People recovering from cataract operations were saying things like 'I'll be able to drive again!' 'I can read this now! I couldn't read it before!'

It was just an ordinary day for this ward, but I felt like I'd fallen into a page of the New Testament. The blind see! God works for the needy. *Every* little thing that is done to relieve human suffering has its first impulse in the heart of God. On average, today, by the measures of extreme poverty, the world is getting better, God's justice is spreading. Through humans—many of them, his own people—he is putting right what is wrong for the poor.

God works on his own timescale. Here is a very humbling thought. His forbearance is meant to bring us to repentance (Romans 2:4). He is patient with us, not wanting any to perish (2 Peter 3:9). Imagine this! The all-powerful God of love and justice at times lets great suffering happen. He hears the cries of the oppressed and he *sits on his hands.* Why? Sometimes he judges it good to wait.

The sandwich

I always find it remarkable that the only things that didn't obey Jesus on earth were humans. At the Master's command, waves collapsed, demons fled, limbs grew, bread multiplied. But humans? He told them what to do and they did something else. There is something incredible about what God will put up with from humans, what disobedience he will face, what injustice he will sit out, in order to win them finally. God waits, and often gets criticised for it.

Other times God seems even to let things move too quickly; the person looking for a happy retirement is struck down too soon. We cannot do anything about this beyond seeking God and trusting him. He is good, he loves mercy and hates injustice, but he lingers around or presses forward according to his own internal clock, not ours. There is a saying in the court system: 'justice delayed is justice denied.' But that is not true in God. He is an eternal being, and so are we. Mortality is delayed in some and hastened in others; it's not fair; but it will be; and beyond understanding God we are called to walk with him: protesting perhaps, but also surrendering, trusting, praising.

There is a day coming. Years ago I drove past a horse and carriage on our roads, a rare sight. The horse was being whipped to trot faster. Its eyes were wide, it was foaming at the mouth, and it was shiny with sweat. Every time I drive on that road I think of that horse. But that was many years ago, and whatever cruelties it suffered are over now. In the same way, we believe there is a day coming when injustice will end for good. The wrinkle has a limit. Peace and justice will be universal. A day is coming.

'God's not fair'

God has entered our pain. In Jesus, God moved himself from the realm of mere academic speculation about fairness and made the argument personal. He has tasted injustice from the inside out. He knows what it is to be sentenced to death by a baying mob, abandoned by a cowardly judge. He knows what it is to be flogged like an animal. God in Jesus is many things, Saviour above all of them, but he is also God's eloquent way of telling us to 'shut up already about injustice.'

What do we do about this?

So what do we do about this?

A stream flows through the Universe and we glimpse it in the Bible.

One picture of it is 'the river of the water of life' flowing from the temple in the closing chapters of the book of Revelation. The same stream appears in the book of Ezekiel, bubbling from the renewed temple, making the salty land sweet. An explanation of it comes from Jesus: 'Whoever believes in me, as Scripture has said, rivers of living water will flow from within them' (John 7:38) and 'the water that I will give [you] will become ... a spring of water welling up to eternal life' (John 4:14).

The stream is God's mercy. It is intended to flow into us--the Church, the new temple--and then out from us into the world. From us it's supposed to broaden into a river delta, so that the whole earth is irrigated. I think it is the main part of the answer to the protest, *God isn't fair.*

While dry argument has its place, I suspect God isn't at his happiest debating lesser beings about justice. He'd rather be out there doing it. That has to be our vision too.

The sandwich

The words 'righteousness' and 'justice' are interchangeable in the Greek, I understand, so it's OK to translate Christ's sayings in the Beatitudes like this:

'Blessed are those who hunger and thirst for justice, for they shall be filled' (Matthew 5:6)

and

'Blessed are those who are persecuted because of justice, for theirs is the kingdom of heaven' (Matthew 5:10).

Is God fair? A stream of mercy pours through the heavens. Those who drench themselves in it themselves become sources of mercy and justice. They set the world back on its feet. The static question has a dynamic answer, one that can catch us up in it and occupy all our creativity and energies. Is God fair? 'There is a river ... come and see what the Lord has done' (Psalm 46:4,8).

WHAT I LEARNT FROM NEARLY DYING

Where to invest
 (2017)

Where in your sickness is the meeting place between really wanting and quietly knowing? Invest there.

Between 2009 and 2013, I nearly died three times. In May 2013, I was in a coma for the best part of a month. When I woke up I was unable to breathe, swallow, drink or go to the toilet without mechanical help. Nor could I move. I was hallucinating and no-one knew if I was brain-damaged.

I spent a couple of years convalescing. High doses of steroids caused my body to swell, damaged my eyesight and gave me symptoms of diabetes. I was kindly pushed around in a wheelchair by my wonderful family for many months. When I started to walk again, I used to grasp my door handle with gratitude after braving the outside world for just a few hundred metres.

At the time, I didn't think we were suffering post-traumatic stress, but for about a year I cried in church every time we sung the old hymns. I couldn't stop myself: those hymnwriters, schooled in more pain than we are, I think, knew to turn sorrow into song.

Eventually I recovered from it all. I know now that experiences like mine are quite common, because medical care is so good, and doctors don't know when to stop. Lots of us come back from the edge of death or will do.

The sandwich

I emerged from these years a different person, as you will or would. It was a landmark in my life, perhaps as big as getting married or turning to Christ. I do struggle to make sense of it and being a writer doesn't necessarily help: we writers might sometimes be guilty of arriving at conclusions prematurely in order to meet a deadline.

But here's (the current draft of) what I (think I) learnt:

- The love of others is astonishing
- Broken is good
- I am not as important as I like to think
- Faith heals you

The love of others is astonishing

First, it was an experience of love. I saw sides to people I didn't normally see. The love and endurance of my family was astonishing. So was the care of some of the medical staff, professional (you'd expect that) but also kind and compassionate.

Also, we became aware of a great network of people praying for us. A great web of prayer surrounds and sustains all of us who are God's people, but usually we don't know much about it. In our crisis, however, the letters, cards, and messages we received lifted that curtain. We saw how surrounded by prayer we were. It is an amazing privilege to be part of the church.

Broken is good

Second, it was an experience of brokenness. All of us spend our lives trying *not* to be broken—to stay happy and whole. We seek this through prayer, wise living, savings, diet, reading *Impact*, and much else. But still, the Lord

What I learnt from nearly dying

Jesus' words are right: blessed are the poor in spirit–the broken.

Brokenness strips you of your pride, smugness and boasting. You might not be achieving anything (other than, say, successfully climbing some stairs or walking to the local shop). These losses can take you back to Christ, just you and him. You have nothing, you are nothing. You might be angry with him or confused about why he seems to be neglecting you. But he still calls you a friend and takes delight in you, and it is hard for that not to lift your spirits eventually.

I am not as important as I like to think

Third, it gave perspective. One of the many things my wife did for me (and it is due to her efforts more than anything that I am still here) was to divert most of my emails. This was wonderful. What a waste of time many of them were. I came to realize that many parts of my career were not worth the bother. Many of the church things we do, also, may not be worth the bother, or at least there may be seasons for doing them and seasons for leaving them undone.

It was a relief to learn that I wasn't really needed, except as a husband and father. This is a good lesson.

Faith heals you

Fourth, God can heal us. The night I went into a coma my lungs filled with fluid. I remember the panic and fear as the medical staff tried to find some way to get me to breathe. I remember asking for our church healing team to anoint me with oil. Yet in all the anxiety of that night I was nevertheless convinced that I wasn't going to die.

The sandwich

I'm not sure how I had come to that point. I had already had a long journey with sickness. In 2011, for example, my heart stopped, my vital signs went to zero and I had to be electrocuted back to life. I have often struggled with fear of an early death. Yet somehow through those earlier difficulties I found comfort and certainty that I would live a normal span of days. That confidence sustained me even in the fear and panic of that horrible night.

This is hard to explain. It is different from really wanting not to die, or being in denial, or just saying something firmly and hoping it comes true. It was (and is) a sustaining, quiet confidence. I wanted to live for just two reasons. In my case, these were my family, and my writing. Somehow I had become convinced I was going to get these two things back, and see good days again, and run my full course. God still had them stored up.

With the best medical care, only 30% of people survive the illness I had. This is worse than getting Ebola. Yet I was so sure I was going to live that I was determined not to die. I think it was a gift of faith.

I have come to think that such gifts are often given to us and that they are key in chronic illness. The question to ask is *'what are you confident you will receive?'* I have observed that some people are desperate to live but don't think they will (and they don't). Other people are oddly confident in something—for example that will see their daughter's graduation. And they do. Their faith heals them.

What I learnt from nearly dying

Here is a helpful question when you are facing death. What's God still got in his hands for you? What are you confident about? Note that I am talking about restful faith, not desperate hope. Where is your confidence, your rest? Invest in that place, I would suggest. Take your stand there. Maybe you are confident you will live another twelve months. Maybe you have faith for further life and service. Maybe you just have confidence that everything is in God's hands, even if you don't understand what's happening.

Or maybe you know you're going to die. If so, take charge of that too. Don't let people soft-soap you. Your faith in God's goodness and purposes will give you steadiness and happiness whether your time is short or long. I think asking God '*what do you have in your hands for me?*' and then leaning into him to receive it is the best advice I have to give--poor and unhelpful as it may be.

***

For a couple of years after I emerged from hospital in 2013, I had a Bible text for the screensaver on my computer. It was to help me take hold of God's promises. It read: '*I will not let you go unless you bless me*' (Genesis 32:26). About a year ago, I was able to replace it with this: '*In my distress I called to the Lord ... The Lord answered me and put me in a wide open place*' (2 Sam 22:7, 20, paraphrased).

God is good.

PRAYERLESSNESS

About catching the moment
(2018)

Didn't have to do much research for this piece. For some reason, I felt I knew quite a lot about the subject already.

Prayerlessness requires real effort on our part.

When the Holy Spirit brushes against your soul, you need to brush him off. When you see a need, you should suppress the desire to bring it to God. When you sense a flame rising in your heart for God or eternity, you must douse it.

Practice, of course, helps. With dedication you can coat your heart with a solid shell that resists most holy urges. But even so, if we are Christians, every day we are buffeted by any number of nudges, longings, sorrows, questions and needs that prompt us to go and find God. It's hard work to dodge them all.

The root cause

I think the reason for our prayerlessness is mostly the same reason that we don't eat a proper diet, read improving books, make that call to a friend, or learn the piano. It's that *in the moment*, we decide to play on our phone or flick through our social networks instead. We say no to prayer when we should be saying yes, or yes to some attractive thing when we should be saying no to it, and the accumulation of thousands of those moments eventually hardens and forms us into what we are and will be: I didn't learn the piano, I didn't look after my body,

The sandwich

and I've just declined my millionth invitation to meet Jesus in prayer.

Yes, we are urged to pray

Do we need to pray? Er, yes:

'Pray in the Spirit on all occasions with all kinds of prayers and requests. With this in mind, be alert and always keep on praying for all the Lord's people' (Ephesians 6:18). 'Do not be anxious about anything, but in every situation, by prayer and petition, with thanksgiving, present your requests to God' (Philippians 4:6). 'Devote yourselves to prayer, being watchful and thankful' (Colossians 4:2). 'Pray continually' (1 Thessalonians 5:17). 'I urge, then, first of all, that petitions, prayers, intercession and thanksgiving be made for all people' (1 Timothy 2:1). 'Therefore confess your sins to each other and pray for each other so that you may be healed' (James 5:16).

Then we notice that Jesus was quite happy to live as a human being, but he did not seem to manage life as a prayerless human being. Sometimes he stayed up late to pray. Sometimes he got up early. Sometimes his disciples just caught him praying. Ministry decisions? He prayed. Healing? Ditto. Feeding thousands? Ditto ditto. Personal crises? In the desert, in the garden, didn't matter. He called on God. He called on God until he was satisfied. You would say there was something of a pattern there.

What if you're too busy?

Perhaps you are too busy?

I refuse to believe anyone is too busy to pray. To my way of thinking, the busiest people most of us ever meet

Prayerlessness

are parents with young children. Babies poop, cry, need comfort, get hungry, get mad and never hesitate to get in touch. They tend not to be all that patient either. Parents of such creatures, especially when not helped by others, are busier than a general fighting a war. Show me a young mum doing most of the caring of two small children and I will show you a sleep-deprived zombie who is too busy to finish a sentence, let alone a meal, and for whom a bathroom break is a triumph of battlefield planning.

And yet she has time to pray. When the kid is sleeping, or plugged onto her breast, or being wheeled up and down a corridor in the pit of night, she has time to reach out to God. Her prayers may not be coherent, but that doesn't matter. Coherence can be overdone. She's slurping an energy-drink at the spiritual ringside, ready for another round.

Honestly, you're not too busy to pray.

So what is the cure?
Is there a cure? There is.

First. Understand you *can* be more fluent in the things of God and prayer. Look around your church. Some people have mastered it. Some people know God and walk with him every day. There are even some people-- plenty of people actually—who are quiet and hesitant in social settings, but when they are switched over to prayer-mode they turn confident and eloquent. When they start to pray these people are like an academic walking into a library or an alcoholic opening a bottle of Scotch. They're home. Heaven is their happy place, even while they keep one foot on earth. You can be a bit more like them.

The sandwich

Second. Understand what happens when you pray and what happens when you don't. To turn to God in prayer is to access a secret, invisible world where you can pull levers that change things on earth and where you can come face to face with Christ.

Missing out on prayer, on the other hand, means that part of us lies forever fallow. Part of us that could be fruitful, colourful, playful, remains unploughed, unsown, and the butterflies must flutter elsewhere. All of us have areas of our life like that: but our prayer life never needs to be one of them.

More than that, if you don't pray you're mostly stuck with earthly solutions to everything. This is not great.

Third. There are a million possible solutions to the issue of prayerlessness. I suggest they all flow from a single principle. *Combatting prayerlessness requires some mixture of discipline and spontaneity.* This is the same way we become fluent in other areas of life, such as keeping fit or learning a musical instrument.

We need to build in some regular habits, but we also have to remind ourselves that keeping up the habit is not the aim. Enjoying God and being with him is the aim. It's like practising the piano. We don't practise so that we can say 'I practised'. We practise so that we can make music.

How do we practise prayer? It surely varies with each individual and each season of life. It's good to find out from other people what does and doesn't work for them. Then see what works for you. Here's my list; your friends will have other lists.

Prayerlessness

1. Schedule a regular time- either a part of a day or a number of minutes in the day. You might start small: ten minutes. Then you might get more ambitious. I have a friend who as a young Christian decided to tithe his waking hours. A tithe of sixteen waking hours is 96 minutes. For some years he aimed, and mostly kept, to the plan of either studying his Bible or praying for 96 minutes a day. Things changed, I am told, when he got married; but it was a good discipline for a long time.
2. If you're married, get into the habit of praying together every day. My wife and I do this every night and we've learnt it's a good habit.
3. Decide that you are going to pray even when the situation is non-optimal. It isn't perfect to pray in the corridor at work as you walk to the toilet; but it's not a bad moment to turn over whatever's on your mind before God.
4. If you can't get alone, write or type your prayers. People will think you are just fooling with your phone.
5. Reclaim your insomnia. Can't sleep? Pray. Stay in bed if you like. So your mind drifts? Well, steer it back. Non-optimal, half-sleepy prayer is better than no prayer at all, like a sleepy kiss is better than no kiss at all. Stop waiting for everything to be perfect.
6. Don't always use words. It's OK just to be in God's presence. Sometimes you don't have words.

The sandwich

7. Alternatively, it's OK to speak words if that helps and it's OK just to pray in your heart if that helps.
8. Sign up for some regular prayer food. This can help broaden your horizons. I recently started working with the Operation World prayer ministry. They have an app that you can access every day and thus pray for the world over a year. Couple of months in, I've kept up. Many groups have similar initiatives.
9. Try things. Pray through the alphabet – pray for something beginning with A, then something beginning with B, and so on. Pray through the psalms. Use the Lord's prayer as a set of headings.
10. Try a total immersion method. If your church has 24-7 prayer room, or prayer event, sign up for an hour and see what happens.

You get the idea.

SHALLOWNESS

How to master looking good on an empty soul
(2018)

This article and the next were prompted probably by the way the Christian faith was a popular choice in Singapore, especially among the young, which has challenges all its own.

Shallowness is a disease that you can catch when you are a new Christian. It can also steal up on you when you are older in the faith. What are the causes and is there a cure? Read on.

The two most famous Bible passages about shallowness are probably the Parable of the Sower and the parable called the 'House on the rock'. They are both about the same thing: someone who looks good on the surface but is stunted underneath. A plant with no root springs up but withers in the sun (Mark 4:1-8). A house with no foundations is impressive until the storms come (Matthew 7:24-27).

Symptoms of shallowness

The symptoms of shallowness can also be found in the healthy. But if we look carefully, we can see a pattern.

Enthusiastic. The shallow person may be enthusiastic. You may even find them a little *too* enthusiastic, suddenly going to lots of meetings, buying things from Christian bookstores, and talking a lot. The shallow are fond of the grand gesture, the sudden commitment. The seed on rocky soil sprang up *quickly*. The house built on sand could have been a show-house, completed on time and under

The sandwich

budget, not at all like the other house, where the builders were still hacking through rock and hadn't poured any concrete yet.

Enjoys the big meetings. Another symptom is enjoying big worship meetings. The music, the beat, the crowds can be inspiring, but they can also be the equivalent of baby-food. Does your Christian life dip between meetings? Do you need another one to fire you up again? Are you, in fact, a baby, living on milk and crying between feeds? The book of Hebrews says 'anyone who lives on milk, being still an infant, is not acquainted with the teaching about righteousness' (Hebrews 5:13).

Busy. Busyness can be a sign of shallowness. My wife, who is a maths teacher, tells me that children are quite happy working through exercises. What do they really hate? Thinking. We Christians can be the same way, keeping busy. Yet we are told to think, to reflect deeply, not to keep skipping onto the next thing: 'whoever looks intently into the perfect law that gives freedom, and continues in it—not forgetting what they have heard, but doing it—they will be blessed in what they do.' (James 1:25).

Chasing the latest fad. We are all a bit faddish as Christians, desperate, perhaps, to find some ingredient that will supercharge our Christian lives. It is a further sad thing that preachers who want to make a name for themselves will exploit this by selling us their books or inviting us to their conferences. These of course can be good. But these things can also be a distraction from taking our own bucket to God for him to fill. Paul warns us in Ephesians not to be 'tossed back and forth by the waves, and blown here and there by every wind of teaching and by the cunning and craftiness of people in their deceitful scheming' (Ephesians 4:14). Faddishness is a symptom of the shallow.

Doesn't have eyes on the prize. The prize is Christ. Yet the shallow are often looking for affirmation and respect from people they want to impress. Kids from Christian homes do this. They love their parents and want to please them, and so they do Christian things. But it's no good having your eyes on your parents rather than Christ. The Bible calls it 'double-mindedness'.

Do we see a pattern yet? The shallow are doing lots of good things, and they can look good, but they are avoiding personally meeting the living God.

Towards a cure

There's a cure. Here are some of the medicines. As with all medicines, they only work if we take them.

Opportunities to obey his voice. One of my lecturers at Fuller Seminary years ago taught that God allows things into our lives that force us to make choices. They may be small things in themselves. But we have to decide, 'will I do this thing?' Or some issue of integrity comes up, no-one will see us, will we show integrity or not? These little-seeming choices are gifts from God, daily milestones in a journey to a greater depth with God. Obeying him is actively choosing between a life of shallowness and a life of depth. He or she who is faithful in little will be trusted with much.

Suffering. Sooner or later, in this world, suffering will enter our lives. We can't do anything about this (apart

The sandwich

from avoiding it if at all possible). But we can choose our response. The book of James says, 'Consider it pure joy, my brothers and sisters, whenever you face trials of many kinds, because you know that the testing of your faith produces perseverance' (James 1:2-3). This astonishing text is a remedy for shallowness, but how does it work? We don't—we can't—rejoice in the suffering itself. Instead, in our suffering, we shift our gaze onto God. God is still good, we remind ourselves, God is excellent, faithful, true, unstoppable in his purposes, unending in his kindness. This small morsel of pain we are tasting cannot be compared with the glory that will one day be revealed. And as we rejoice in God in the face of suffering, down grow the roots, down into God.

Choosing the humble path. Since shallowness is all about show and impressing others, try the humble path. Put your light on early in the morning and go seek God when no-one is watching, just you and him and the Bible. Give some money away that no-one knows about. Swallow your tongue when you'd like to snap back at someone. Allow people to criticise you without defending yourself. You may be misunderstood or exploited, but you'll go deeper with God. 'It is good for a man to bear the yoke while he is young.' (Lamentations 3:27). (I think it's true for women too.)

Waiting. I often think that God has got his timing wrong. I look at situations and think, 'why doesn't God do something?' People are frustrated and unfruitful. God seems to operate on a different clock, a slow one. Yet waiting can drive us deeper into his loving arms. It can lead us to desire him, him supremely, not just the thing waited for. If we cooperate and worship him, God's delays can be a therapy for the shallow. 'I wait for the LORD, my whole being waits, and in his word I put my hope' (Psalm 130:5).

Focus. That great Christian writer Philip Yancey has written recently that he doesn't find it as easy to read books as he used to. He blames the internet, and how easy it is to click from one story to another. This is scary: it's a path for deep thinkers to become shallow ones. The internet is like having a pizza restaurant in our bedroom. We can snack anytime. We have to find ways to resist the pizza sometimes and eat some proper food, otherwise we'll become that unpleasant thing, the old, shallow Christian, who hasn't learnt or repented or changed their mind since sometime in the last millennium. 'Not that I have already obtained all this,' wrote Paul, 'or have already arrived at my goal, but I press on to take hold of that for which Christ Jesus took hold of me' (Philippians 3:12).

Silence. Have you ever tried simply being silent before God? I do wonder, sometimes, if God just wants us to shut up. Perhaps you wonder the same thing. 'The LORD is good to those whose hope is in him, to the one who seeks him; it is good to wait quietly for the salvation of the LORD. ... Let him sit alone in silence' (Lamentations 3:25-26, 28).

So: shallowness is a disease. But hand in hand with God, and with effort on our part, we can be led into the depths. We can have deep roots and solid foundations; we can weather the storms and be a blessing to many.

'I NEVER KNEW YOU'
About not living on fumes
(2019)

Two passages in the New Testament record people's shock when they are shut out of the Kingdom of God at the last day. They can't believe it. In one passage, people complain, 'We ate and drank with you, and you taught in our streets!' (Luke 13:26). In the other, they go even further: 'Lord, Lord, did we not prophesy in your name, and in your name drive out demons and in your name perform many miracles?' (Matthew 7:15-23).

'I don't know where you are from,' Jesus says to those who lived in his neighbourhood. 'I never knew you', he says to those who worked spectacular miracles in his name. What does he mean?

In both these examples, things look fine on the surface, but underneath, there's nothing.

More of the same

Plenty of other places in the Bible talk about situations where people looked good for a time, or even worked miracles in Christ's name, but shared the same deep lack. They were running on fumes, not on steady supplies of fuel.

- Judas Iscariot went with the other disciples on preaching tours, healing and driving out demons. He looked just like a proper apostle but was always a thief and was found out in the end.
- In Ephesus, some Jewish exorcists tried casting out demons in the name of Jesus. It worked until

The sandwich

one day they were mauled by a demonized person and barely managed to escape alive.
- In the Old Testament a prophet for hire named Balaam prophesied accurately about the people of God, but money rather than God owned his heart. The New Testament warns us several times of Christian-era Balaams (see 2 Peter 2:15 and Jude 11).

Frequently, the Bible warns us against people who look good but are in fact, bad. 'Watch out for false prophets. They come to you in sheep's clothing, but inwardly they are ferocious wolves' (Matthew 7:15). Beware 'false apostles, deceitful workers, masquerading as apostles of Christ' (2 Corinthians 11:13). 'They are blots and blemishes, revelling in their pleasures, while they feast with you' (2 Peter 2:13).

Knowing and being known

Jesus says to all these surprised people, who looked so good, 'I never knew you.' What does he mean? And does he mean us?

1. It can't mean that there is anything God doesn't know about us. He is God. He's measured our shoe size, counted the hairs on our head, heard every word of our self-talk. He knows when we meant well. He knows when we say we meant well but really didn't. He knows everything about us and judges it with an utter fairness. Every good point we might want him to consider - he will already have listed it. Everything we'd rather he hadn't seen – he will have seen that too. We

'I never knew you'

   are entirely exposed to him, even if we would
   wish to cover some bits up.
2. Yet there is another sort of knowing. Stalkers
   turn knowing about someone into a criminal
   obsession; but perhaps they are hungry for
   another kind of knowing and of being known,
   which they never enjoy or find. All they know
   are facts; all they are known as is as a pest. They
   never experience the heart-to-heart knowledge,
   the relational knowledge, the mutual openness,
   with another person that Jesus also seems to
   mean when he says, 'I never knew you.'

This companiable, heart-to-heart knowing is a two-way thing. Paul puts it like this to the Galatians, 'Formerly, when you did not know God, you were slaves to those who by nature are not gods. But now that you know God—or rather are known by God—how is it that you are turning back? (Galatians 4:8-9). Jesus says simply, 'I am the good shepherd. I know my sheep and my sheep know me' (John 10:14).

This opening of the heart to the Other, to God, is what some of us so strenuously avoid. I can go along with the Christian crowd. I can even get involved in all kinds of spiritual fireworks, impressing everyone with the show, just don't let me face him heart to heart, naked and unarmed. Let me keep busy in his name instead. Or let me just gingerly tread around him and his call, keeping a respectful distance: 'Oh yes, I know him well, I'm quite familiar with the teaching.'

This is such a huge theme of the Bible. Adam hides behind a tree, not a brilliant strategy when the one looking

The sandwich

for you is All-Seeing. 'These people honour me with their lips but their hearts are far from me' says Isaiah, quoted later by Jesus, and identifying a later group of Adams sheltering behind a tree of religiosity (Mark 7:6 NIVUK).

'Here I am!' Jesus says to the smug and all-knowing Christians of Laodicea. 'I stand at the door and knock. If anyone hears my voice and opens the door, I will come in and eat with that person, and they with me' (Revelation 3:20). *Don't hold me at a distance, cool and sardonic and flip. Face me. Meet me.*

Knowing is trusting is following

This heart-to-eart knowing, this relational knowledge, is bound up with trusting. If you are emerging from your hiding place, laying down your weapons, taking off your headphones, and facing God defenceless, argument-less and alone, then necessarily you are trusting him to deal with you kindly and well.

Necessarily you are also committing yourself to do what he says. So another way of looking at 'knowing' is 'trusting and obeying'. This is God's 'solid foundation': 'But God's solid foundation stands firm, sealed with this inscription: "The Lord knows those who are his," and, "Everyone who confesses the name of the Lord must turn away from wickedness"' (2 Timothy 2:19).

It is a surrender. That is why it is so simple and so terrible. It is why (I think) the biggest barrier between anyone knowing God and being known by him is not ignorance but pride. God can take a humble person a long way even if they have just a few sandwiches in their mental lunchbox; a proud genius with all the world's information on a smartphone will still be blundering in the

'I never knew you'

dark. Pride makes us stupid, but humility lets us see and know.

But when you surrender, when you trust and follow, knowing him and being known, there is healing for your wounds, rest for your tired bones, comfort for your sorrows, forgiveness for your rebellions and stubbornness, energy for your serving, and quietness and happiness and glory.

LET IT BE

About the tangle of free will and love, and the weakness of God.
(2020)

Many of the world's problems are blamed on God giving us 'free will'. I'm not sure that God would be as heartless as that.

Does God force us to do things? If so, does he bypass us, or squash us to get his way? Does that show a lack of respect? Does it contravene 'free will'?

Before we go any further, let's not talk any more about 'free will', as if we were all independent actors with plenty of access to information, not influenced by our peers, able to make good choices on our own with our own resources.

I don't believe it. I've yet to meet anyone like that. We peer at life through a soup of prejudice that distorts what we see. We are influenced by the networks of people around us, the tribes we belong to. Once we've made up our minds on something, we tend to defend our turf, accepting facts that bolster our view and rejecting the facts that don't. Arguably our tendency to rebel against the light of God and choose our own dark corner makes us still more half-witted. We humans are dim. We don't get it. Free choice would be spoilt on us.

All sorts of things can make us a bit less slow of mind and thick of head. We could listen to others; admit we might be mistaken; test our ideas against evidence or logic. Perhaps when we are younger, and know less, and the

The sandwich

world is open to us, our brains are more plastic and we are more open to learning. But still.

Then imagine you are God. OK, it's probably unimaginable but imagine yourself with perfect knowledge, in perfect light, looking down on these bumbling toilers on earth, blundering, grumbling, bumping into one another. Their bodies are extensively wired to feel pain and you watch their neural systems light up as they injure themselves and each other, and then go back and do it again. To God, it seems, we look 'harassed and helpless, like sheep without a shepherd', and he has compassion on us (see Matthew 9:36).

I don't think God's biggest problem looking down on this scene, if we can so speak, is a lofty analysis of freedom of choice or free will or the rights of humans. It is about how to get stuff done, among these creatures whom you cannot not love and whom you want the best for.

So for example if God arranges for you to meet *that* girl at *that* event at *that* time and she gives you *that* shy smile and he knows you are *that* sort of person and she is *that* sort of person and you then fall in love and create a happy life together, did he force you? Or was he just smart and kind?

Or if he quickens your torpid soul with life, unblocks your ears, restores your spiritual sight, and you see Jesus for the first time not as some historical artefact but as the Living One and a friend and redeemer; if God unwraps your graveclothes and you stand before him blinking in the sunlight, where in all that was your freedom and choice? Something greater than freedom and choice was here.

Let it be

I was in a coma for a month once and it took my family and the doctors two weeks to wake me up – two weeks of my family talking to me, reading my books to me, of doctors changing the meds. I had no choice in the matter: I was hallucinating about a three-country trip to Africa (which honestly still lingers in the memory though it never happened). In a sense, the love and care of those around me superseded any issues of freedom of choice. They knew I wanted to live again and love again and they fought for me when I couldn't fight for myself. I wonder if that principle ever crosses God's mind and ever governs his behaviour?

The Biblical data is fascinating. Jesus, God's selfie on earth, showed respect and restraint to those around him, often at cost to himself. He wasn't coercive or controlling. He gave instructions that were disobeyed but he didn't sulk. 'See that you don't tell this to anyone,' he said to the healed leper, 'but go, show yourself to the priest...' Get the medical and judicial proof that you are not infectious so you can rejoin your community. 'Instead [the man] went out and began to talk freely, spreading the news. As a result, Jesus could no longer enter a town openly but stayed outside in lonely places' (Mark 1:45-46). The ex-patient's folly caused Jesus problems, which Jesus had to manage. At no point did he fell the man with a fiery dart. ('I told you – go see the priest! Bam!') Fevers, illnesses, demons, wind and waves all obeyed Christ's words but people didn't -- and at a certain level the Lord seemed OK with that.

Yet at other times, God appears rather more forceful. Jonah is ordered to Nineveh to preach repentance. Nineveh was Israel's enemy and God wanted to bring them light. Jonah buys a ticket for the opposite direction.

The sandwich

God interrupts the journey with a storm. Jonah is then conveyed by various transport modes back to the shores around Nineveh: first, a short flight (he is thrown into the sea), then a longer trip by sea-creature (carried in the hold). He does not like this, but he does repent. When he finally walks into Nineveh, the repentant preacher preaches repentance and to his great disgust his preaching stops Nineveh being destroyed by God's wrath. God gets his way. Nineveh turns to the light. But even then (according to the Book of Jonah at least) God is still concerned with Jonah and his continuing grumbles.

God was also quite forceful when he manoeuvred things so that the gospel burst from its Jewish flowerhead and seeded around the world. The book of Acts, chapter 10, tells how the apostle Peter fell into a trance, lost an argument with God, had a timely meeting, made a journey to some pre-prepared Gentiles, preached a short and perhaps tactless sermon, but it was enough for the Gentiles to have their own Pentecost at Cornelius' place. Along with plenty of other actions God made the light go global – which was a win. Along the way, Peter and others changed their minds about whether non-Jews should get grace: another win. Letting Peter argue had helped.

Consider these various examples. They share a common thread. God appears to have largely got his way. *But there is a weakness in God's strength.* Or to put it another way, God's strength is made perfect through God's 'weakness'. What did the storm achieve in Jonah? Repentance. What did the trance and the events at Cornelius' house achieve in Peter? Repentance, a fresh turning to God and a willingness to believe God for new and greater things. What did Jesus seek from giving people on earth a liberty to obey him or not – a liberty he

Let it be

didn't give demons, fevers or storms? He provided space for repentance and often people took the offer up.

From our limited perspective, then, it seems that many of God's actions, and many of what seem like his lack of actions, focus on winning the person as well as winning the day, rather than either philosophical high-mindedness or the need to control. We aren't told what happened to the healed leper. We don't know if sometime afterward, perhaps years later, he reflected on Jesus' treatment of him, the power and the meekness, and turned to the Risen Christ in love and wonder. Perhaps he did; perhaps he didn't; but he wasn't short of data, or insight, or opportunity.

What shall we say then? God's foolishness is wiser than our wisdom and his weakness is stronger than our strength. His patient tread is faster than our hurry. One day, says Ephesians, everything will be brought to complete unity in Christ: the whole created order will be renewed, humanity along with it. When we read that along with the rest of the Bible we are brought to conclude that many, many individual humans will repent and unite their ways with God's ways, and (as other passages teach) others will not repent and will finally lose all their footholds in life and love. Meanwhile we are in the hands of One whose patience achieves more than human impatience; whose grace promotes deeper obedience than human laws. God is not like the government, passing laws and issuing fines. His kindness unclenches our fists and is an ointment to our sore eyes. God's action among us is still a mystery. But the glimpses tell us he is extraordinary in his character and that shows in the way he uses his power.

AND FINALLY

When we left Singapore, a friend gave us a framed cross-stitch she had painstakingly sewn. It read:

Dear Glenn and Cordelia

Have faith and trust in the Lord

His mercy and love are everlasting

It hangs in our bedroom still, a quarter of a century later, a reminder of the kindness of friends and the straightforwardness and strength of Singaporean Christianity, as well as of the faithfulness of God. Despite working for a magazine called '*Impact*', we hardly made one ourselves; but we were so enriched by our time there.

ABOUT THE AUTHOR

Brought up in West Yorkshire in the UK, Glenn has had home addresses in London, Côte d'Ivoire, Los Angeles and Singapore, but has settled with his wife in Cambridge, UK. They have two grown-up children.

Glenn has a batchelor's degree in physics and a master's in Christian mission. Unlike the rest of his family, neither of his degrees is from Cambridge University and so he is considered a slow learner.

He enjoys cafes, curries, board games and his hammock.

To hear about new books and free offers, go to glennmyers.info. He blogs at slowmission.com. He's also erratically on Goodreads, Facebook and Twitter.

OTHER FIZZ BOOKS BY GLENN MYERS

More than Bananas: How the Christian faith works for me and the whole Universe.

A freewheeling personal exploration of how the Christian faith can make sense in the face of science, suffering, injustice, and God's apparent affection for three-toed sloths.

Your book is wonderful! I do hope that it is very widely read.

Prof. Sir Colin Humphreys CBE FRS, Cambridge University

Bread: Taking hold of what really matters

Adversity or difficulty helps us focus on what is important: what is bread for our souls. This book helps us find what really matters to us, ideally without suffering the adversity first.

NOVELS – A TRILOGY

Paradise – a divine comedy
The Wheels of the World
The Sump of Lost Dreams

Next to our world is an invisible realm, where our human souls mingle alongside good and evil spirits, moods, half-formed opinions, forgotten melodies, fairground rides and deadly traps: the 'heavenly places'.

Jamie Smith and Keziah Mordant nearly kill each other in a car accident, then find that they can commute between earth and the heavenly places. Captured, experimented on, freed, then coached by an Old Testament prophet and a crusty female physicist, they take up a new job: shaping history by fixing souls. Fuelled by the gourmet food of the heavenlies, diverted by Jamie's memories of his former girlfriend Caroline, and usually wanting to kill each other, Jamie and Keziah stumble uncomprehending into what life might really be all about: love dripping through the craziness.

A hysterical surrealist take on what is out there after life on earth, or next to life on earth, or simultaneous with life on earth, or whatever. A story of Gods in kilts, crystal clear memories, and walls made of our pixelated fears. Delightful. Jeannette M, Goodreads